Marvelous Mini Quilts for Foundation Piecing

Including: Practice Tree Ornament Block and nine blocks featured in nine mini quilts
Plus..."Tornado" - Medallion Sampler Quilt using all nine blocks

Table of Contents

Make Perfectly Marvelous Minis

Why Are We Doing This?

Well, I can think of five reasons to make these wonderful little quilts using Foundation Piecing...they're EASY to make, they're ECONOMICAL because they require few supplies and very little fabric, they're ADDICTIVE - you'll find that you can't make just one, they're PORTABLE - you can carry the whole quilt in your pocket, and they're FLEXIBLE because you can use these little blocks on shirts, dresses, skirts, as borders on bigger quilts or for cornerstones, etc. (Also they're not fattening). I started to make these out of curiosity after a friend said that she had just finished a Snail's Trail quilt made of 3" blocks. Wow, I thought, how did she manage to cut, mark and piece such itty bitty blocks?!?! Then she told me that she hadn't made a single template, did not have to mark any fabric, wasn't trying to line up the seam allowances on microscopic triangles—well, I think you get the idea!

The idea of using paper or "waste" fabric as a base for piecing is not new. Our mothers, grandmothers and great-grandmothers used newspaper for both string piecing and "English piecing" and muslin (or in the case of a quilt that I have, mattress ticking) for crazy quilt foundations. Nowadays, our lives are so busy that we simply can't make all the bed-sized quilts that we want to make and the idea of making smaller quilts has become quite popular. The first time I tried to make a miniature quilt, I cut out tiny templates and tried to position them on the fabric so I could mark around them. Oops! They were smaller than my thumb and I couldn't quite keep the template still and mark around it at the same time. Using a fabric or paper base with the STITCHING lines marked right on the base, solved the whole problem! I have a cute little basket with several projects in it —when I'm sitting by the side of the __________ (fill in your child's favorite sport's activity location), waiting at the doctor or dentist's office or sitting around chatting with friends, I can sew these little blocks. I am also a dedicated machine piecer and quilter so in my little quilts, I intermix both machine and hand pieced blocks—the technique is virtually the same for either medium.

I would love to own every fabric ever printed (and my husband claims that I am well on the way to succeeding), but of course this is expensive and space-consuming. Doing minis allows me to buy small amounts - fat quarters - of lots of different fabrics, use them in a quilt and still have plenty left over. It also lets you use up the dribs and drabs of fabric from larger projects—pieces that are too big to throw away and yet too small to do much with. You'll find that your definition of a "usable" scrap will suddenly include pieces as small as 1 1/2".

I am sure that you will find, as I did, that this technique is absolutely addictive. The blocks make up quickly and before you know it your mini quilt will be finished. These little blocks are also perfect for decorating clothing, place mats, hand towels, etc. The blocks pieced on muslin bases have all the seam allowances sandwiched between the front of the block and muslin backing—the only visible raw edges are around the edges of the block.

Organization

Let's talk about how this book is organized. The first few sections are general information—supplies, general techniques, etc. Please read them! In order not to bore you to death, I'll try not to repeat myself endlessly. You will also find items labeled ***"I.D.'s"***—these are Important Digressions—hints and helps that are more general in nature but that can make your (quilting) life easier; **"Punch Lists"** which are reviews of the major items in a section (shown in shaded boxes); and the occasional ***"R.R.R."***—Rosintoski's Rules of the Road.

Following the general information are the patterns and directions for the quilts. These are arranged generally speaking in order of difficulty so that the techniques build on each other. Feel free to make the last quilt first, just promise to read over the information for the other blocks first.

Supplies

By Hand

All you need for hand piecing are needle and thread, a glue stick, a small pair of sharp scissors, the muslin bases for the blocks and some scraps. I have a small basket with these items in it and a little decorated tin box (that used to hold candy) for my "trash"—the trimmings from my seam allowances. I use a "sharp" size 10 needle for hand piecing but any reasonably thin needle will work. I am very particular about the thread I use and both hand and machine piece with cotton or a good quality long staple polyester. Size 50 cotton thread is, once again, generally available, although any good quality thread will do. Because you will be piecing both light and dark fabrics together a neutral color thread—perhaps a khaki or medium gray—works well. If you are piecing blocks that are all in one color family using a medium tone of that color is a good choice.

***I.D.**—The higher the number on the spool of thread or the package of needles, the thinner or finer the thread and the smaller the needle, which, of course, defies all logic. Speaking of thread ... thread "sews" in lighter, so when you are trying to match thread always select either an exact match or a half shade or shade darker. Also if you can, lay a piece of the thread, rather than the whole spool, on the fabric to see if it matches.*

By Machine

The most important thing when you are piecing or quilting by machine is a sewing machine that has been cleaned and oiled and is in good working order. So if you have never cleaned the bobbin area of the machine or oiled it, now is the time! Haul out the old machine manual (yes, I know reading the manual is boring) and see what you have to do. Can you remember the last time you changed the needle? If you can't or the needle is almost as old as you are, treat the machine to a new needle. A size 12 or 14 (80 or 90 in metric) universal or sharp needle is what I recommend—do not use a ballpoint needle. Wind one or more bobbins with neutral thread (beige or khaki) and thread the top of the machine with a darker color (black or dark gray). Please use a good quality thread—your machine will be much happier and so will you!

If you are planning to sew on paper bases, now is a good time to experiment with your stitch length. Take a piece of paper—I use computer paper, copier paper, or notebook paper (use crummy paper rather than good, heavyweight paper) and draw a few straight lines on it. Set your stitch length down around 1 or a little above 1 (about 23 - 25 stitches to the inch) and sew down the line. If the paper is well perforated and you can tear it apart easily, but it does not simply fall into two pieces all by itself, you have the right stitch length! If you will be machine piecing on muslin, ignore all this and just use a regular stitch length—about 12 to 14 to the inch.

***I.D.**—When I took my first formal sewing class, the most important thing I learned was to MAKE NOTES! As I have gotten older (but not smarter) I have found this to be invaluable advice. My instructor gave me "permission" to write in my patterns and books. So right now, before you do anything else, write down your stitch length ____________.*

Miscellaneous Supplies

Keep an indelible pen (sometimes called a laundry pen) with your supplies to mark bases with information about color and fabric placement. (More about this later.) You will also need a glue stick, a small pair of sharp scissors and a pair of paper scissors (if you are piecing on paper).

Fabric Selection and Preparation

A new project is always the perfect excuse to visit all the fabric stores and buy a lot of new fabric; on the other hand, these projects are perfect for using up your leftover scraps from other projects (let your conscience be your guide). I prefer to use 100% cotton fabric in my projects although I have been known to throw in a little of this and a little of that from time to time. Unless you are planning to wash your mini quilt, there is no particular need to prewash your fabric. I prefer to machine piece on unwashed fabric because it has more body. If you are hand piecing and having difficulty with some of your fabrics, go ahead and wash them. If some of your fabrics seem wimpy, try spray starching them. Always wash and dry the muslin you will use for your bases.

***I.D.**—OK, let's spend a moment on the issue of prewashing (or not prewashing). I don't prewash a lot, but I maintain a healthy skepticism! Any fabric from a manufacturer that I never heard of before (look at the ends of the bolts and the fabric selvages when you buy); solid reds, browns and greens; very bright colors where the fabric feels stiff; and any prices that are too good to be true make me very suspicious! The first thing I do is to cut off a little piece of the fabric and drop it in a glass of cool water (I wash all my quilts in cold water, if you wash in warm or hot water use that) and set it on the kitchen counter. After awhile I wander back and look to see if the water is still clear. If it is, then I put the wet scrap on a piece of muslin and iron it dry with the hottest setting on my iron to see if heat transfers any color. (Recently, I have heard about some cases where fabric that washed without running transferred dye in the dryer!) If the water is not clear, then I wash the whole piece of fabric and dry it along with a piece of muslin to see if it transfers color. If you have doubts, don't use it! If you usually prewash all your fabric, please continue to do so.*

It is very difficult to tell you exactly how much fabric you will need for a project, although you will find fabric estimates for each quilt. If you are making scrappy quilts, just gather up your scraps and arrange them by color or sort into light, medium and dark piles. You will, of course, need bigger pieces for the borders and you will find those yardages in the patterns sections. If you belong to a quilt guild or sewing group, a fun thing to do is to have a scrap swap. In my guild, we each made up packets of 20 different 3" squares (we made 25 of these packets) and all traded with each other—each of us went home with 500 squares and interestingly enough there were very few duplicates! Another group I am in traded 1 1/2" by 10" strips - we sent four of these to each of 30 people.

Fabric Pattern And Color

Because the pieces that you will be using in these blocks are so small, you might think that only very small prints will work. Actually, large prints also give interesting results. Medium/small prints where the motifs are about 1/2" or larger sometimes look strange when cut up into these small pieces. To "test drive" a fabric, cut a window template. Cut a small triangle and a small strip (about 1/4" to 3/8" wide and about 1 1/2" long) out of the middle of an index card or stiff piece of paper (no accuracy required here!). Lay the card on the fabric...move it around...see anything you like? Fabrics with very scattered patterns sometimes tend to look like solids.

Color choices and usage are major stumbling blocks for many quilters. This is the time to break free of the restrictions that you have placed on yourself. Force yourself to try colors in ways that are new and unusual. When fabrics are placed next to one another surprising things can happen—several bright fabrics which are real "screamers" separately may calm down and look pleasing when used together; beautiful fabrics which are wonderful when viewed alone may disappear when put in a block. Do a little reading on color theory and the color wheel to gain some background and then experiment. Blocks which look like they have curves in them but don't, like the Snail's Trail, won't "spin" if made with all medium-colored fabrics. One way to test the effectiveness of fabrics before going to the effort of actually constructing a block, is to make a mock up. Simply draw the block on a piece of paper and glue stick down scraps of fabric, then back off and look at the block to see if it "works."

Every quilter has "trouble" with certain colors and color combinations—I don't do well with browns, golds and greens. For a long time, I solved that problem by simply not using those colors. Now, I force myself to buy fabrics in those colors and to try to use them in my quilts. I still don't use them frequently, but "sometimes" **is** an improvement over "never."

RRR*—Forget everything you ever learned about colors "not going together," but don't wear brown shoes with a blue suit.*

In any case, after you have selected the fabrics, simply sort them into light, medium and dark piles and if you are using scraps, pop them into little plastic bags.

Getting Started

Choices for Bases

Muslin

The quality of the muslin that you use for your base will affect the entire project, so find a good quality muslin. If you shop at a quilt store, they will help you select your muslin. If you shop at a chain store, carefully examine the available muslin. If it is very stiff and coarse you will not be happy! Look for 100% cotton muslin which is drapeable yet not wimpy. (I realize I just told you not to buy stiff muslin and not to buy soft muslin which sounds contradictory, but if you put the various brands of muslin side by side and feel them, you will see a definite difference!) If you simply can't find any muslin that seems right, buy white or cream lightweight solid cotton broadcloth. You should be able to get about 40 or so blocks from one yard of muslin.

Paper

Any available paper can be used—left over computer paper, copier paper and notebook paper are all fine. Actually, you don't want to use "good" paper because it can be harder to remove. Just experiment with whatever you have handy.

Interfacing, Stabilizers and Other Stuff

You may want to experiment with non-woven interfacing and some of the newer tear-out stabilizers that are currently on the market. Keep in mind that fabric and stabilizers will remain as part of your quilt and that paper and "tear-aways" will have to be removed without breaking your stitches!

In summary, if you use a muslin or fabric base, it becomes a permanent part of your quilt. The advantages of muslin are that it can be sewn by hand or by machine, it adds body to your quilt and it adds stability to your patches if you are using non-traditional fabrics such as lamé, satin, rayon, etc. The major disadvantage is that it adds another layer to quilt through if you are planning to hand quilt.

Using paper or a removable base pretty much limits you to machine piecing. It can be very tedious as well as messy to remove and if you have used very scant seam allowances, you have to be very careful to not fray your fabrics. On the other hand, it is cheap, does not stretch and makes hand quilting easier.

I use both muslin and paper bases for my quilts and find that both work well. So experiment and see what you like best!

Making the Bases

Heat Transferring the Block

The easiest way to mark bases for foundation piecing is by heat transferring the block. Complete instructions for heat transferring with iron-on transfers, as well as quilt block transfers for all the quilts in this book, can be found in *Iron-On Transfers for Foundation Piecing Mini Quilt Blocks*, ASN #4159.

Tracing

To trace the block pattern, tape pattern to a hard surface and use a ruler and permanent pen. ***Note:*** *Trace pattern onto tracing paper first if you cannot see design through your base.* I find it easier to use short dashed lines or even dotted lines. Remember to copy the numbers and letters. If you are tracing a nonsymmetrical block from one of the block patterns, remember that your block after it is pieced will be a mirror image of your base! (Please see Mirror Images on page 5.)

I.D.*—We all fall into the same trap when making transfers or marking quilt designs—we try to make the lines more and more perfect and darker and darker! Remember the ONLY person who needs to see the transferred design is YOU and you only need to see it at a distance of 12" to 18". I have found that when tracing quilting or block patterns that if I use a dotted or dashed line, I am more accurate and leave less ink/*

chalk/marker on the quilt or muslin base. No one is going to grade you on your transfers!

Transfer Pens and Pencils

There are several brands of transfer pens and pencils available. If you experiment with them, make sure the pencil has a sharp point and that you draw the thinnest possible line. Again, I use a dotted or dashed line. Check accuracy of your lines after transferring. Sulky® makes a good Heat Transfer Pen. Try to draw your lines using the minimum amount of ink necessary to get a good impression. Experiment with the amount of time that you need to press to get the design transferred! Every iron is different. If you want to use a transfer pen or pencil for paper, make a sample and make sure that the transfer ink does not smear.

Paper Perforating

Here is a quick way to make several paper bases at a time. Trace or transfer one copy of the block onto paper. Stack two or three pieces of paper; pin or staple together. Unthread your sewing machine, use a size 14 or 16 needle (90 or 100), use a regular stitch length and "sew" down each line of the block pattern. Make sure to pierce a hole at each corner of each patch. You can also perforate one sheet of paper and rub "pounce" or finely powdered chalk through the holes to transfer the design to the base. I personally have never had much success with this method, but it is a method of transferring quilting patterns that has been used for years—our grandmothers and great-grandmothers used cinnamon for marking light fabrics and flour or cornstarch for darks. (Beware, the chalk or cinnamon does not stay on very long).

Other Methods

There are various brands of dressmaker's carbon available, some are permanent, some are not. I am sure that by the time you read this, new methods of transferring will be available. I'm a gadget and notions nut, so I usually buy every new thing that looks interesting and give it a try. And last but not least, I draw my patterns on the computer and then print to paper or muslin. It is possible to print to muslin if it is ironed to freezer paper. You have to baby your printer along to get it to accept the muslin without revolting, but it can be done.

Regardless of the method that you select, make sure that the block design is accurate, that the ink is permanent on the base and that it does not wash into your fabric!

Mirror Images

Several of the blocks that we will be making are not symmetrical—that is to say that either the "left" side and the "right" side or the top and the bottom are not identical. Many blocks that are strongly diagonal or that spin are not symmetrical. In this book, the blocks which are symmetrical include the Square in the Square (page 43), Broken Dishes (page 44) and the Pineapple (page 38). Because we are sewing on one side of the base and placing our fabric on the other side of the base, what you see on the printed side of the paper or muslin base is not what you get on the fabric side.

If you are in imminent danger of getting a bad headache by even considering this subject, just remember that consistency is what is important. Let's take the House as an example. If you look at **Fig 1**, you will see the House opposite (the mirror image) of how it appears in the Sampler (page 54). So, when you are making a quilt that consists solely of repeats of one block pattern make sure all the bases look the same before you start. If you really want all your wheels to spin to the right, for example, and are not quite sure that you know what the printed base should look like, try this little trick. Prepare one paper base on thin paper (tracing paper works fine here) and color the patches on the unmarked side with colored pencils or magic marker. Does it spin in the desired direction? If it does, terrific! Make the rest of the bases. If not, you will have to mirror image the drawing and color another sample.

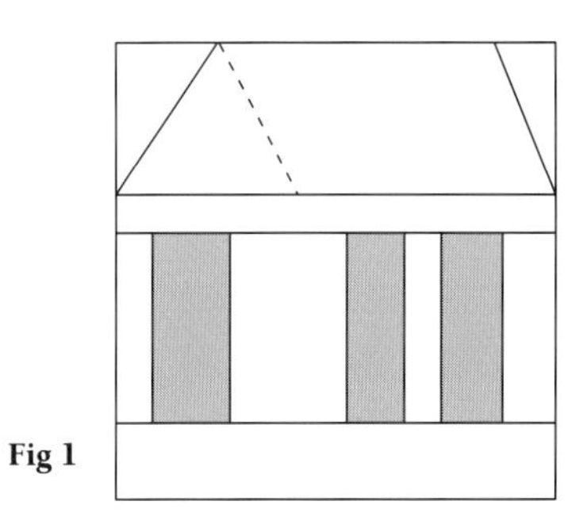

Fig 1

General Directions

What do all those numbers on the Block patterns mean?

The numbers indicate the order in which the patches are placed and sewn on the base. If you don't follow the numbers, it won't work.

What about seam allowances?

Use between 1/8" and 1/4" seam allowance for patches and 1/4" seam allowance around the edges of the blocks. As you construct a block, you will find a seam allowance that is comfortable for you. If you are using a fabric that seems to have a bad case of the "unravels," leave a full 1/4". A general rule of thumb is: the smaller the block and the smaller the pieces, the scantier the seam allowance.

What about grain lines?

The pieces that you are using will be so small that the whole issue of grain lines really doesn't matter unless the pattern on the fabric will look very odd (like a little geometric that travels over the edge of the patch) or, in the case of some solids, where the grain line is very obvious. (Time for that window template on pages 3 and 4 again!) It doesn't hurt to try to have the lengthwise or crosswise grain on the patches at the edges of the block.

Precutting the pieces

When you first start making these blocks, you may find it easier if you have "precut" some of your scraps. Look at the block—if it uses strips (log cabin, chevron, etc.), measure the width and length of the longest strip and cut a few pieces that are about 3/4" longer and wider. If the block uses triangles, cut a few rectangles that are 1" longer than the longest side of the triangle and 1" wider than width of the triangle. If the block uses squares, well, you get the idea. You will waste a little fabric by doing this, but I find that it leads to fewer "oopsies" and less ripping out. (I hate to "unsew"!) This also gives you pieces big enough to handle easily.

Placing the first patch

The most important thing to keep in mind, is that the fabric patches go on the unmarked side of the base and that you are going to sew on the printed line. So, find #1 on the block and cut a piece of fabric bigger than that piece (see above). Put a tiny bit of glue stick on the unmarked side of the base. Hold the base up to the light with the printed side facing you and place the first patch with the fabric right side up and centered on the unprinted side so that you have a seam allowance on all sides, **Fig 2**. (This is easier to do than to read about!)

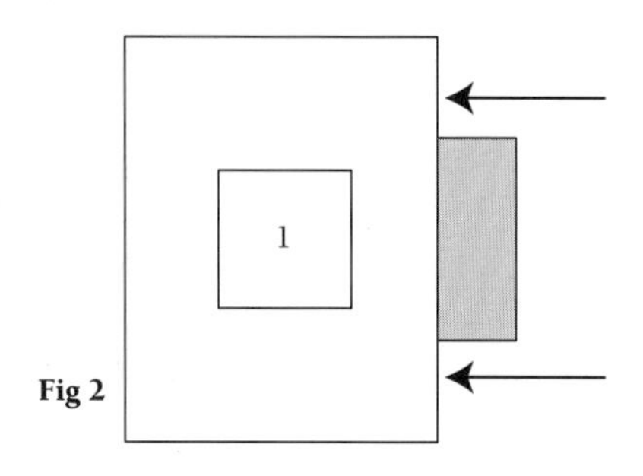

Fig 2

Pre-trim - the secret to success

Because we are using scraps and roughly cutting out our patches, the shape and size of the patch will vary. I have found that by trimming my seam allowance before I sew (pre-trimming), my patches align better and I make fewer mistakes. Holding the block with the *printed side towards you,* fold the paper or muslin base towards you along the printed line between patches #1 and #2, **Fig 3** (machine stitchers will fold 1/4" above the printed line). You should see the *wrong side* of the fabric from the first patch sticking up. Trim this raw edge to a scant 1/4". *This is your seam allowance.* Unfold the base and turn it over. Place the fabric for the second patch, ***right side down*** with its raw edge aligned with the seam allowance that you just pre-trimmed, **Fig 4**. It is generally not necessary to pin. As a matter of fact, I happen to find that pins usually get in the way more than they help. Pick up the block and get ready to sew on the line between the two patches. We will continue this "pre-trimming" as we add more patches. As you pre-trim and add patches, there will be odd looking pieces of fabric sticking out here and there. Don't panic! They will all disappear eventually!

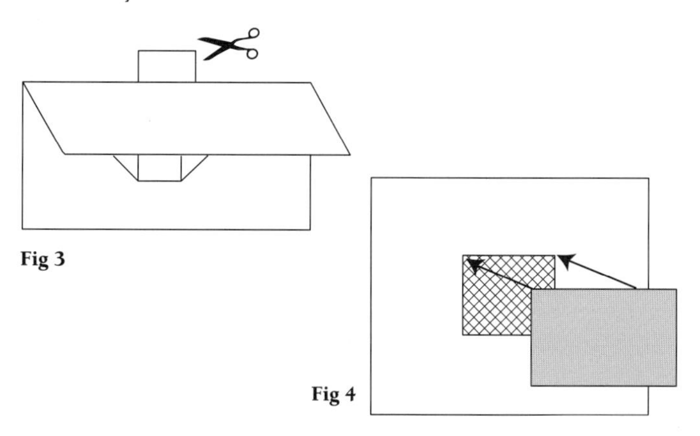
Fig 3

Fig 4

Sewing By Hand

How to start and end a patch

You may knot your thread or take several back stitches to anchor the thread. Start sewing exactly at the beginning of the line and sew to the end using a small running stitch. I back stitch every four or five stitches. Sew tightly enough so that the thread doesn't show on the right side of the block when you open the patch up but not so tightly that you are gathering the muslin base. End your line of stitching with a knot or several back stitches. Smooth open the patch you have just added and finger press or gently iron.

Moving from patch to patch

Make sure that the previously added patch has been smoothed open. Hold the block with the printed side facing you and fold it back on the line between the patch just added and the next patch; pre-trim the fabric edges which are sticking up. Turn the block over; lay the next patch right side down with the raw edge aligned with the pre-trimmed seam allowance, **Fig 5**; sew and smooth open. Continue adding patches to the block following the numbers.

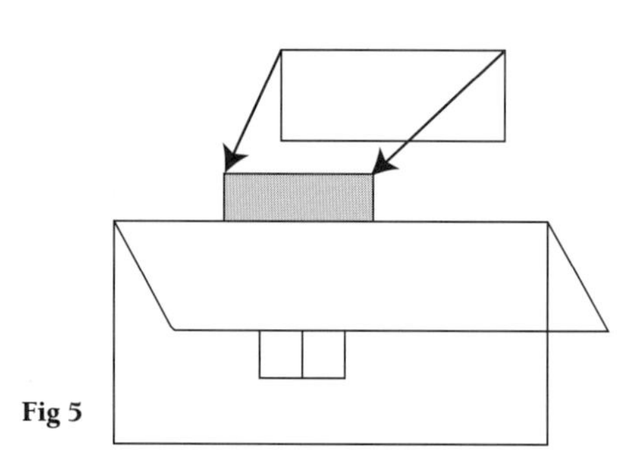
Fig 5

When you have added all the patches, press gently, turn the block printed side up and carefully trim the outside edges to 1/4" seam allowance. By the way, I have found it very helpful to leave a full 1/4" seam allowance around the outside of the block even if I have been trimming the individual patch seam allowances to less than 1/4". It will be easier to sew the blocks together if you have a full 1/4" seam allowance and you can always trim the block seam allowances after the quilt top is assembled.

Sewing By Machine

Why you shouldn't back stitch

I rarely back stitch when sewing by machine because I have found that it sometimes leads to "lumps" or stitching that is not exactly on the line. I start stitching about 3 to 5 stitches (or a scant 1/4") before the beginning of the sewing line and end my stitching the same amount past the end of the line, **Fig 6**.

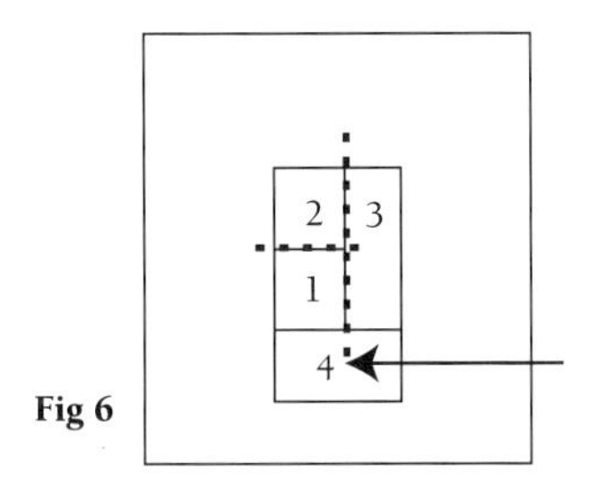

Fig 6

There are a few special situations where your life will be easier if you do back stitch and they will be pointed out as they occur. By starting your stitching before the start of the patch and ending past the end of the patch, you will find that *it is impossible to fold the base towards you on the printed line for pre-trimming!* Don't panic—when machine stitching, I fold the base *1/4" above the stitching line and trim the raw edge even with the fold.*

The only thing that you have to concentrate on here is remembering to be consistent! When machine stitching, *always fold the base 1/4" above the printed line for pre-trimming,* **Fig 7**. (Yes, in real life we all sometimes fold exactly on the line and trim off the entire seam allowance - oops! There is not much that you can do other than rip out the offending patch and replace it!)

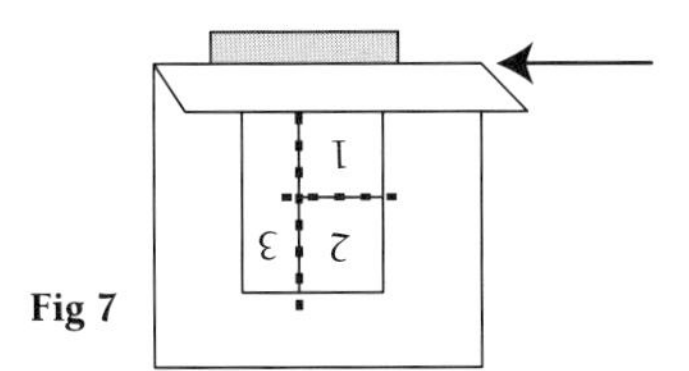
Fig 7

If you are sewing on paper and your paper base is falling apart as you sew, slightly lengthen the stitch. The paper will take a remarkable amount of abuse! Even if you have to rip out a seam and the paper totally perforates along a line it will still be fine. Just don't do what I did the other day. I accidentally tore off a piece of the paper base and so I taped it back together. Then forgetting that I had put tape on it, I proceeded to iron the block with a nice hot iron. Tape does not take well to being ironed and I had melted tape on the ironing board and iron.

While the temptation to remove the paper as soon as you have finished piecing a block is all but irresistible—restrain yourself! Leave the paper in until you have assembled the quilt. After you sew two blocks together, remove the paper only from the seam allowances so that you can press them. Leave the rest of the paper in to keep the block stabilized.

Pressing

You can finger press a newly added patch open or press with an iron—just be gentle. (I am firmly convinced that leaping up and down from the sewing machine to the iron should be considered a valid form of exercise.)

Making a Practice Piece

What a dilemma! What to make first? Well, if you are not too confident of your hand piecing skills or are not on friendly terms with your machine, I suggest that you try one or two of the Tree Ornaments (page 8) first. Otherwise you may choose to jump right into one of the quilts. The Log Cabin (page 12) or Chevron (page 17) make good first projects because the block piecing is not too difficult even though the blocks contain many patches. The Chevron blocks are only 2" in size, however, and you may want to try a larger block first just to become more familiar with the technique.

Tree Ornaments - Practice Blocks

Shown in color on page 35

Special Techniques:

Detailed directions for making your first block

Finished Size:

3 1/2" by 4 1/2"

Please read all of the directions below before you start! They are extremely detailed and cover all of the techniques needed to successfully piece on a base.

OK! Transfer one of the Tree blocks to paper or muslin using one of the methods described in Making the Bases, page 4, gather up your scraps and supplies, take a deep breath and let's make a block.

Supplies (all fabric requirements are approximate)	
Tree fabric	4 1/2" square of fabric or six scraps about 1 1/4" by 3 3/4"
Background fabric	two scraps 2 1/2" by 2 1/2", two scraps 4 1/2" by 2 1/2"
Tree trunk	one scrap 1" by 1 3/4"
Batting and backing	4" by 5" piece of each

Notes:

1. These little trees are fun to embellish so you may want to gather up some beads, bits of ribbon and lace and fabric paints.

2. If you are piecing by machine and have not cleaned and oiled your machine, changed the needle and wound a bobbin...now is the time to do it!

3. Please read all the directions before starting.

4. Remember, this is fun!

Assembly Directions

1. If you have not roughly cut your fabrics to the dimensions in Supplies, please do so now. These dimensions are generous and will waste some fabric, but they give you patches that are large enough to hang on to.

2. You will be sewing on the printed side of the base and your fabrics will be placed on the unprinted side. This will seem a little strange at first but in no time at all, you'll be an expert!

3. The numbers indicate the order in which the patches will be added, **Fig 1**. The tree trunk is the first patch, then the background on either side of the trunk, then the tree itself and finally the background behind the tree.

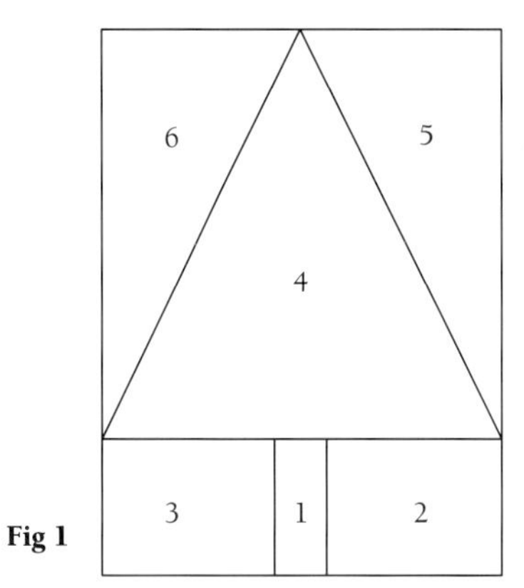

Fig 1

4. Place a tiny dab of glue stick on patch #1 on the unprinted side of the base. Hold the base with the printed side facing you and place the tree trunk fabric on the unprinted side with the fabric right side up, **Fig 2**.

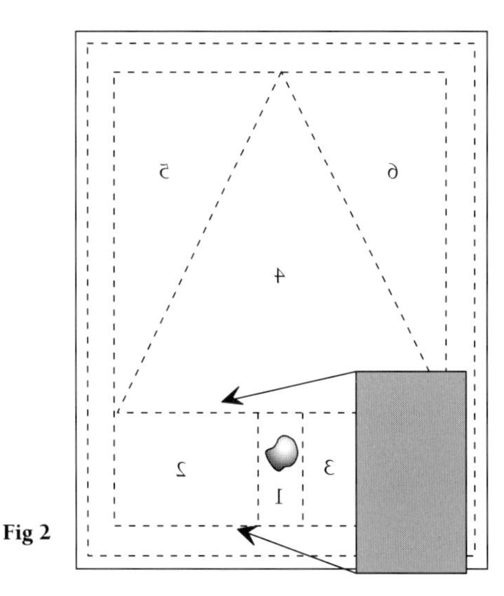
Fig 2

If you hold the base up to the light, this is easier to do. Make sure that you can see fabric sticking out all around patch #1 into the surrounding patches—these are your seam allowances! Make sure that you have at least 1/4" seam allowances—anything larger than that will be cut off as we progress. Placing the first patch is the hardest part of the process and you may have to fuss with it a bit.

5. If you are sewing by hand fold the base towards you on the printed line between patch #1 and patch #2. If you are sewing by machine, fold the base a scant 1/4" beyond the line (this fold is actually in the patch #2 space). You should see the fabric from the tree trunk sticking out. If you don't see tree trunk fabric either your patch #1 is too small or your patch #1 is not positioned correctly!

I.D.**—If you are wondering why I make this distinction between folding the base on the line if sewing by hand and 1/4" above the line if sewing by machine, you will see as you make more blocks that when sewing by machine most of the time you cannot fold the base on the line but must fold it 1/4" above the line! I have found that if I am consistent in what I do, I minimize my opportunities for creative crises! So I always lay out my strips from left to right and sew them together from right to left when I strip piece and stack blocks together in the same order when carrying them to the sewing machine, etc.. I really, really hate to unsew (rip out)! I also write myself lots of notes—unfortunately I do scatter these around and can never find them when I need them, but that's another story entirely. So while necessity may be the mother of invention, I have found that consistency is the mother of sanity. **Note: Be sure to always fold base a scant 1/4" beyond line when you are sewing by machine.

6. Pre-trim. If you folded on the line, trim the fabric which is sticking up to 1/4" above the fold, **Fig 3**; if you folded above the line, trim even with the fold being careful not to cut into the base. I have found that pre-trimming helps me to line up the patch that is being added and prevents me from accidentally cutting off my seam allowances.

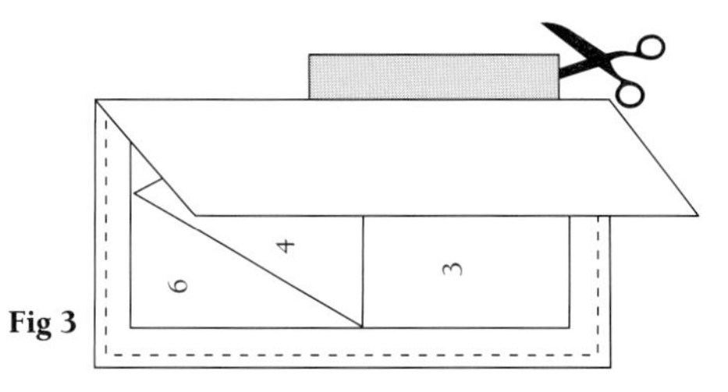
Fig 3

7. Pick up a piece of background (2 1/2" by 2 1/2") and lay it right side down on top of the trunk fabric with the raw edge aligned with the pre-trimmed raw edge of the trunk, **Fig 4**. Sew on the line between patch #1 and patch #2. If you are hand sewing, knot (or back stitch) at the beginning and end of the sewing line. If you are sewing by machine, start sewing three or four stitches before the beginning of the printed line and end three or four stitches beyond the end.

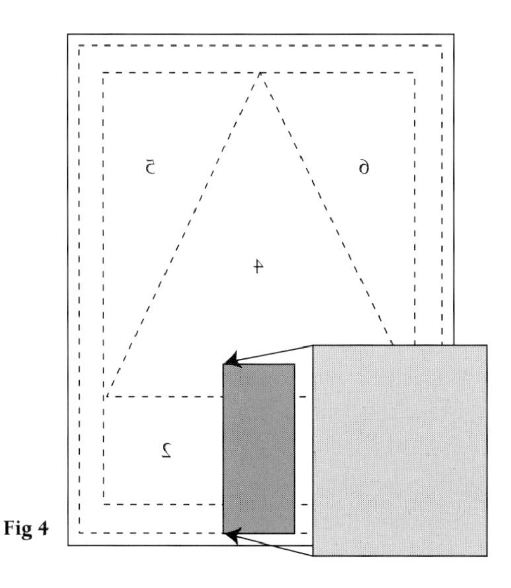
Fig 4

8. Smooth patch open that you just added and either finger press or gently iron. Hold base up to light (printed side towards you) and make sure that you can see fabric for seam allowances extending all around patch #2. If you don't see fabric for seam allowances, remove patch and sew it again.

9. Fold base towards you on line between patch #1 and patch #3 (the other side of the tree trunk) and pre-trim. Place the fabric for patch #3 right side down on top of patch #1 with the raw edges aligned and sew on the line between #1 and #3. Smooth open, press and check for seam allowances.

10. Fold the base towards you on the line between patch #4 and patches #1, #2 and #3 as above and pre-trim. If you are making a one-fabric tree take the 4 1/2" square of tree fabric and place face down on the previous patches and align the raw edges. If you are making a multi-fabric tree take one of your tree strips and place it face down with raw edges aligned. Sew on the line. Smooth open. Check for seam allowances.

11. If you are making a multi-fabric tree, fold on the line between patch #4 and #5. Stop! It is very easy to accidentally fold the base on the line you have just sewn and to cut off the patch you just added! So check and make sure you are folding on the **next** line to be sewn not the one you have just sewn. Pre-trim and add the next strip of tree. You will have all sorts of extra fabric sticking out to the left and the right, **Fig 5**—ignore it! This will be cut off when we add the side triangles which form the rest of the background. Continue adding tree strips until all 6 strips have been added.

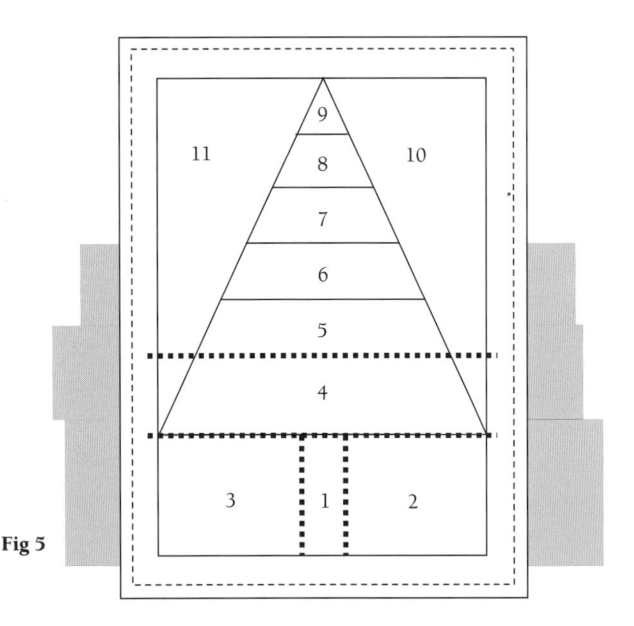

Fig 5

I.D.—*Let's stop for a minute and talk about triangle patches. Most people (including me) have found that they have a great deal of difficulty trying to cut triangles the right size and shape and that the larger the triangle, the harder it is. The easiest way to deal with this problem is to not cut triangles at all but to cut squares and rectangles instead. Squares and rectangles are also big enough to handle. This wastes some fabric, but I believe you will find it much easier! The way that I figure how big to cut a rectangle is by measuring the longest side of the triangle (in this case down the side of the tree) and then from that side across to the point (the corner of the block) and then add 3/4" in each direction. As you become more familiar with the technique you may decide to roughly cut triangles instead of rectangles.*

12. Fold the base towards you on the line between the tree and the triangular background (single fabric tree between patches #4 and #10; multi-fabric tree between patches #4, #5, #6, #7, #8, #9 and #10) and pre-trim the side of the tree. Center the background right side down over the tree, raw edges aligned and sew on the line. Smooth open, press and check for seam allowances. Add the last piece of background in the same way.

13. Wow! You have made your first block! Did it take you longer to read the directions than to make the block? Turn the block printed side up and trim base and fabrics carefully along the dotted outside line.

14. **Finishing the tree:** I love the way these little trees look with the batting showing! Simply layer your backing right side down, your batting and your little block right side up (remove paper); sew 1/4" in from edge of block either by hand with embroidery floss, perle cotton or decorative thread; or by machine using a straight stitch, zigzag or decorative stitch. Trim backing and batting a tiny bit larger than block. If you wish to have finished edges on the ornament, follow directions in Birds of a Feather Chevron, page 20, for an envelope finish or apply a separate binding, (see page 59). Decorate with paint, fancy stitching, ribbons, sequins, charms, lace or anything that suits your fancy.

- The fabric patches are placed on the unprinted side of the base.
- The first patch is placed right side up.
- The fabric edges of the first patch overlap the printed lines to give you adequate seam allowances.
- One edge of the first patch has been pre-trimmed.
- The fabric for the second patch is face down with the raw edge aligned to the first patch raw edge.

Finished Tree Block

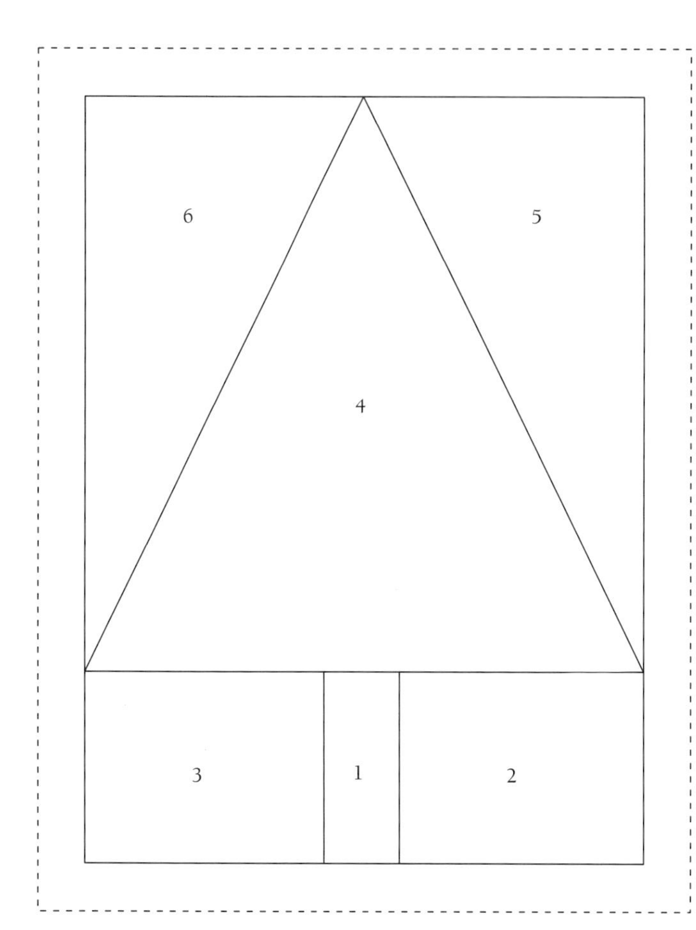

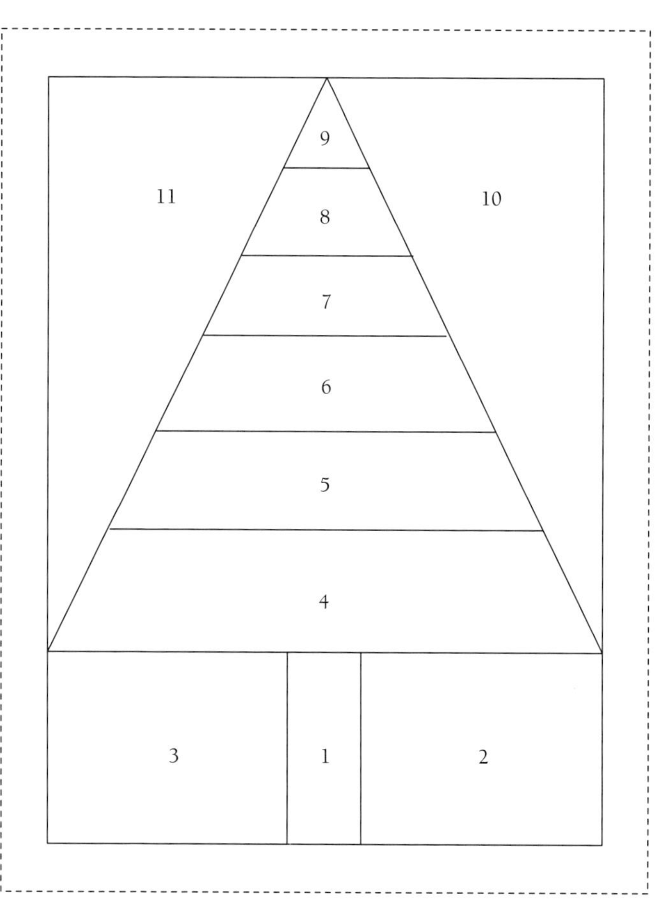

Tree Quilt Block

"Rain, Rain Go Away" Log Cabin

Shown in color on page 33

Special Techniques:
Log Cabin Border

Quilt Size:
12 3/4" by 12 3/4"

Block Size:
3" square

I think there are probably more Log Cabin quilts made than any other quilt. And for good reason! I truly believe that it is impossible to make a "bad" Log Cabin. No matter whether you use a controlled color scheme, every color in the rainbow, new fabrics, old fabrics, big blocks, little blocks, fat logs, skinny logs...it's hard to turn out less than a masterpiece!

R.R.R.*—You are an artist, fabrics are your paints—and don't believe anyone, including yourself, who says it isn't so.*

I called this little quilt "Rain, Rain Go Away" because it reminded me of being a little girl and looking out a rain-streaked window into the woods behind the house. All the hand-dyed fabrics used in this piece are from Shades Studio. I had one piece with all the mottled greens, reds, blues, purples in it and a few other scraps of blues ranging from lights to darks. The little centers are a pale yellow, which is a very traditional color for the center of a Log Cabin.

My main fabric had so many colors and so much "movement" that I decided not to try to segregate the lights to one side of the block and the darks to the other—which is the traditional way to use your fabrics. The setting for the photographed quilt uses an A block and a B block and was inspired by an antique quilt in the Pilgrim/Roy collection. The contrast between the fabrics in my quilt is so slight, that at first glance you can't really see the way the colors are placed in the block. If you were to use higher contrast fabrics with all the lights on one side of the block, mediums on the other side and a dark color in the logs which form the "squares" you would have a very strong graphic result. (Try this with colored pencils on the coloring diagram, page 16.) On the other hand, the traditional coloration for a Log Cabin block is shown in **Fig 1**.

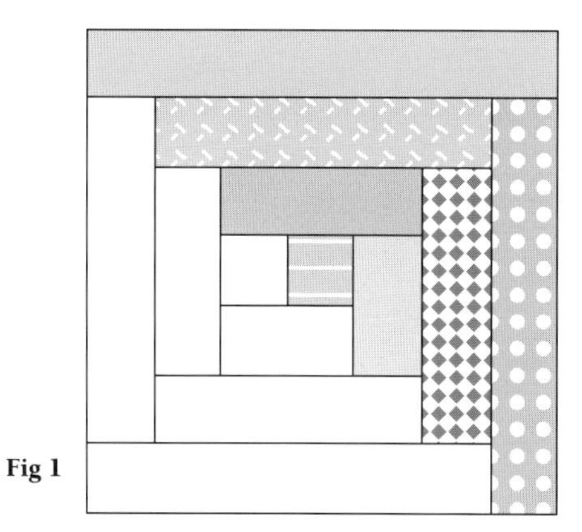

Fig 1

So either gather your scraps and divide them into dark and light piles; or pull out that wonderful multi-hued fabric that you have been saving and didn't know what to do with; or go buy some hand dyed fabric; or even dye some yourself and let's make a quilt!

I.D.*—Let's think about contrast for a moment. There are various types of contrast—color (red/green); intensity (dark/light); pattern (small/large)—and without conscious thought you recognize quilts that have contrast. They're the ones which grab the viewer and say "look at me." There are many books, quilting as well as art books, that discuss color and contrast. Here are some ways to quickly check for contrast in your quilt. If you are nearsighted (as I am) take off your glasses, back up from the quilt, squint and if it's one big blur then it has no contrast. Get a piece of red acrylic (I cut up a report cover from the stationery store), back up and look at the quilt—this drains the colors from the fabrics and helps you to see your fabrics as darks, mediums and lights (this works especially well with solids). Take little pieces of your fabrics or a "paste-up" block and copy them on a copier; if you have an instant camera and can find black and white film, take a picture; use a reducing glass. The purpose here is to stop looking at the colors of the fabrics and to try to see only the contrast between the fabrics. Unless you are making a quilt where it is obvious that the contrast is very high or very low, it can be an unpleasant surprise to finish a quilt and discover that it "just lies there." So, do some reading about color and contrast and try a couple of the tricks above, soon you'll be looking at quilts and fabrics in a new way.*

Even though the Log Cabin block has thirteen pieces, it is probably the easiest of the blocks to piece. Just make sure that all your bases look the same.

Prepare nine muslin or paper bases by your chosen method.

Supplies for "Rain, Rain Go Away" (all fabric requirements are approximate)	
A fabric	1/8 yds-1/4 yd "special" or dominant fabric or equivalent scraps
B fabric	1/8 yd or equivalent scraps
C fabric	1/8 yd or equivalent scraps
Block Center	nine 1 1/4" squares of contrasting fabric
Borders	1/4 yd

In case you want to make a mini Log Cabin using traditional color placement here are the fabric requirements.

Supplies for a traditional Log Cabin (all fabric requirements are approximate)	
Light fabric	1/8 yd or equivalent amount of scraps
Dark fabric	1/8 yd fabric or equivalent amount of scraps
Block center	nine 1 1/4" squares of contrasting color
Borders	1/4 yd

Notes:

1. The assembly methods for both the traditional Log Cabin and the photographed quilt are identical. The only differences are in the color placements of the fabrics.

2. You may find it easier to roughly precut a few logs—cut a few scraps 1" by 1 1/2" for the innermost logs; a few 1" by 2 1/2" for the second round of logs; and some 1" by 3 3/4" for the third round. These are generous measurements, so if you have some real small scraps, don't worry about it, you'll be able to fit them in.

3. Cut squares about 1" by 1" for the centers of the blocks.

4. Make a sample block before you cut up all your fabric.

Assembly Directions

1. Using coloring diagram on page 16, decide which patches are going to be which fabrics (lights, darks, etc.) and color in a little sketch of the block. I mark color placements on bases using a permanent pen to keep lights and darks where they belong. I used to write things down on little scraps of paper, but then I could never find them again.

2. With the printed side of the base facing you, place small dab of glue stick on the unprinted side in the middle of the center square. Hold the base up to the light and place the square of center fabric right side up on the unprinted side making sure that you have a seam allowance all around. The glue stick will keep the patch from shifting.

3. With the printed side of the base towards you, fold the base toward you on the printed line between #1 and #2 (or 1/4" above the line if you are machine sewing) and pre-trim the raw edge of the fabric to 1/4", being careful not to cut the base or move the patch.

4. Following the numbers on the base, place the first log fabric face down on center patch making sure that raw edge aligns with the pre-trimmed edge of the center, **Fig 2**.

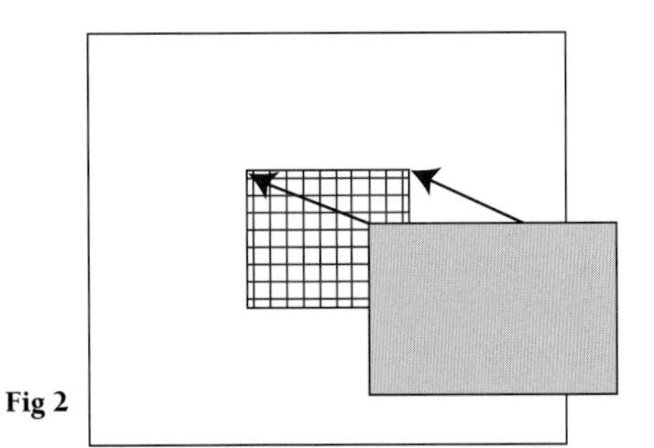

Fig 2

Hold the base to the light to make sure that the log patch overlaps the center patch leaving a seam allowance on both sides. Sew on the line between #1 and #2. Smooth the log open and finger press or gently iron.

5. Fold the base towards you on the line between #2 and #3, pre-trim and place the next log with raw edges aligned. Keep adding logs following the numbers. Remember—pre-trim, align, sew, smooth open—that's all there is to it.

6. If you are making the pictured quilt, you will make five A Blocks and four B blocks, **Fig 3**. If you are making a traditionally-colored Log Cabin, make nine blocks with consistent color placement of your lights and darks.

Fig 3

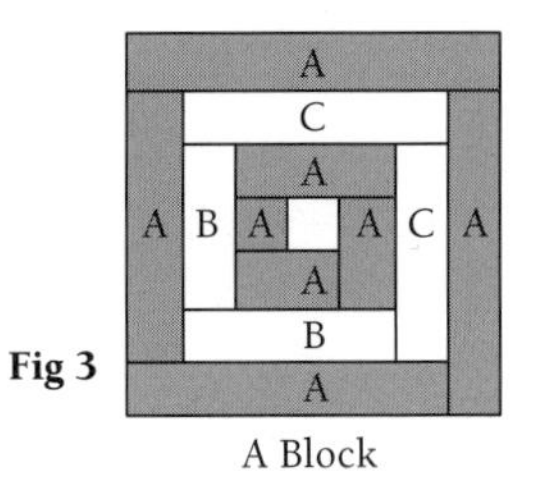

A Block

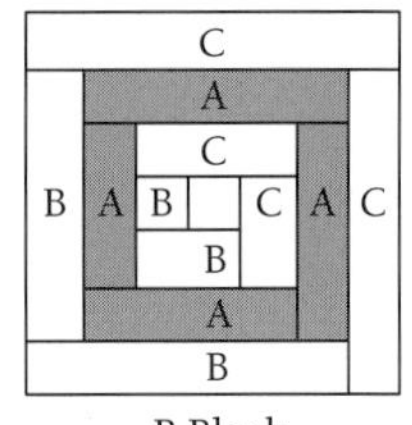

B Block

7. Lay the blocks out in three rows of three blocks. For the photographed quilt (page 12), Rows 1 and 3 have an A, B, A sequence and Row 2 has a B, A, B sequence. If you chose to make the traditional light/dark Log Cabin this is the fun part! There are so many possibilities for Log Cabin sets! Move your blocks around and play with some sets, **Fig 4**. ***Note:*** *Two of the settings in* ***Fig 4*** *require sixteen blocks instead of nine.* Sometimes I have so much fun doing this that I hate to actually make a decision and sew the blocks together!

Use 9 blocks

Fig 4

Use 16 blocks

Use 9 blocks

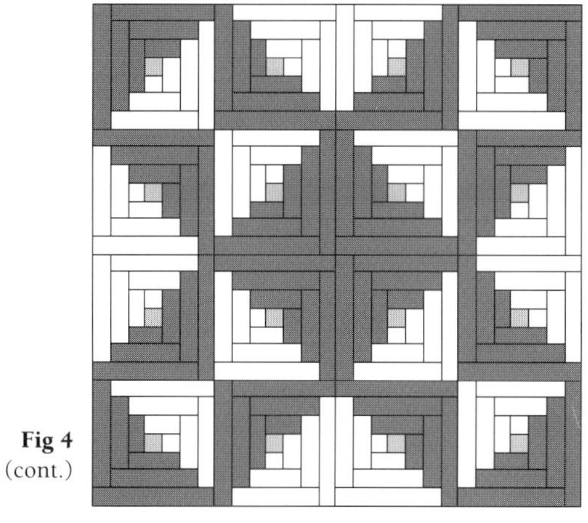
Fig 4 (cont.)

Use 16 blocks

8. Square up each block leaving a 1/4" seam allowance all around; sew blocks together.

Log Cabin Border

When I made the border for "Rain, Rain Go Away," I decided to add the borders the same way I made the blocks—by lapping each border strip over the one before it, **Fig 5**. I added the left border, then the bottom, then the right side and finally the top. You can do your borders this way or in the more traditional way. I cut my border fabric fairly wide (2 1/4") for a quilt that has blocks that are 3", but I just loved that fabric! Experiment! There is no right answer to the question "how wide should my border be?"

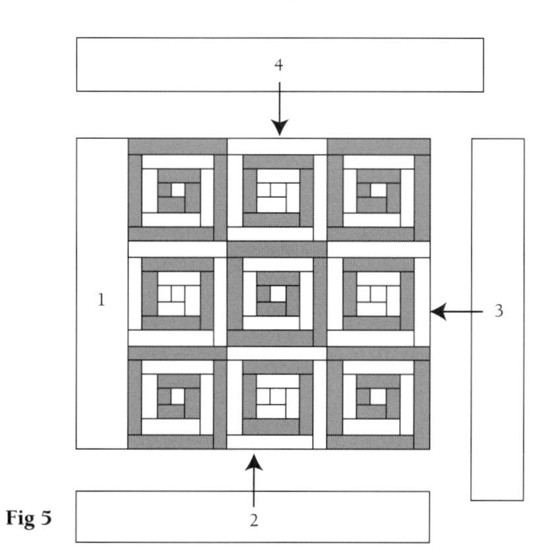

Fig 5

***R.R.R.**—If you like what you are doing, keep doing it. It's the right thing to do!*

- Make sure that all your bases look the same before you start and that you know where the dark and light fabrics will be placed.
- Remember to: Pre-trim, align raw edges, sew, smooth open.
- You need enough fabric for seam allowances! Check after you place each log. It's easier to rip out now, than to have to remove two or three pieces! (Actually it's easier not to rip out all, so check and double check before you sew each piece.)

Finishing the Quilt

Refer to Finishing Up, pages 59 and 60 to finish your quilt.

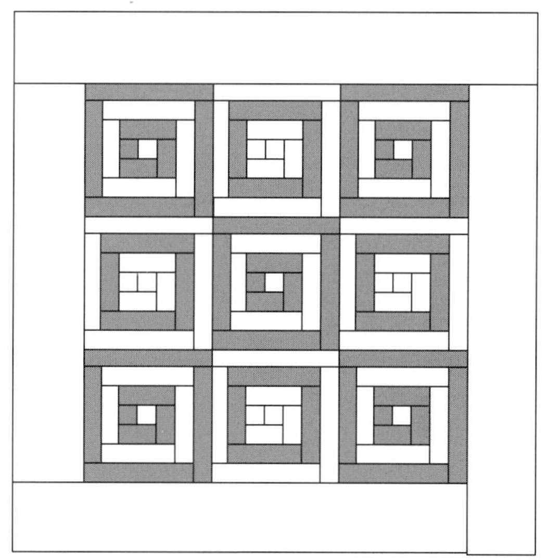
Quilt Layout for "Rain, Rain Go Away"

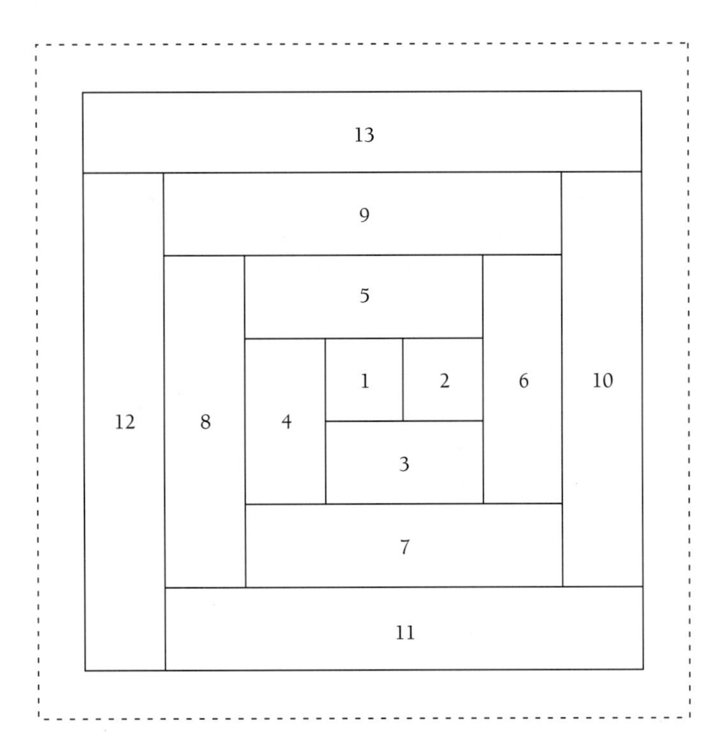

Quilt Block for "Rain, Rain Go Away"

Coloring Diagram

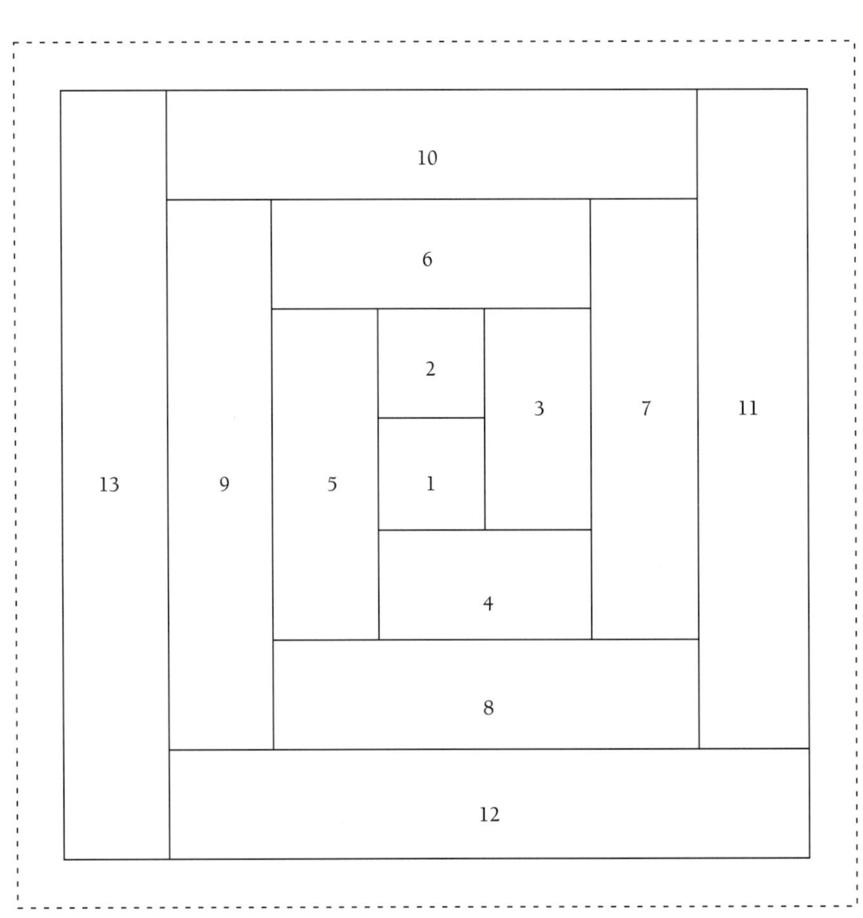

Quilt Block for "Tornado" - Medallion Sampler, page 54

Birds of a Feather Chevron

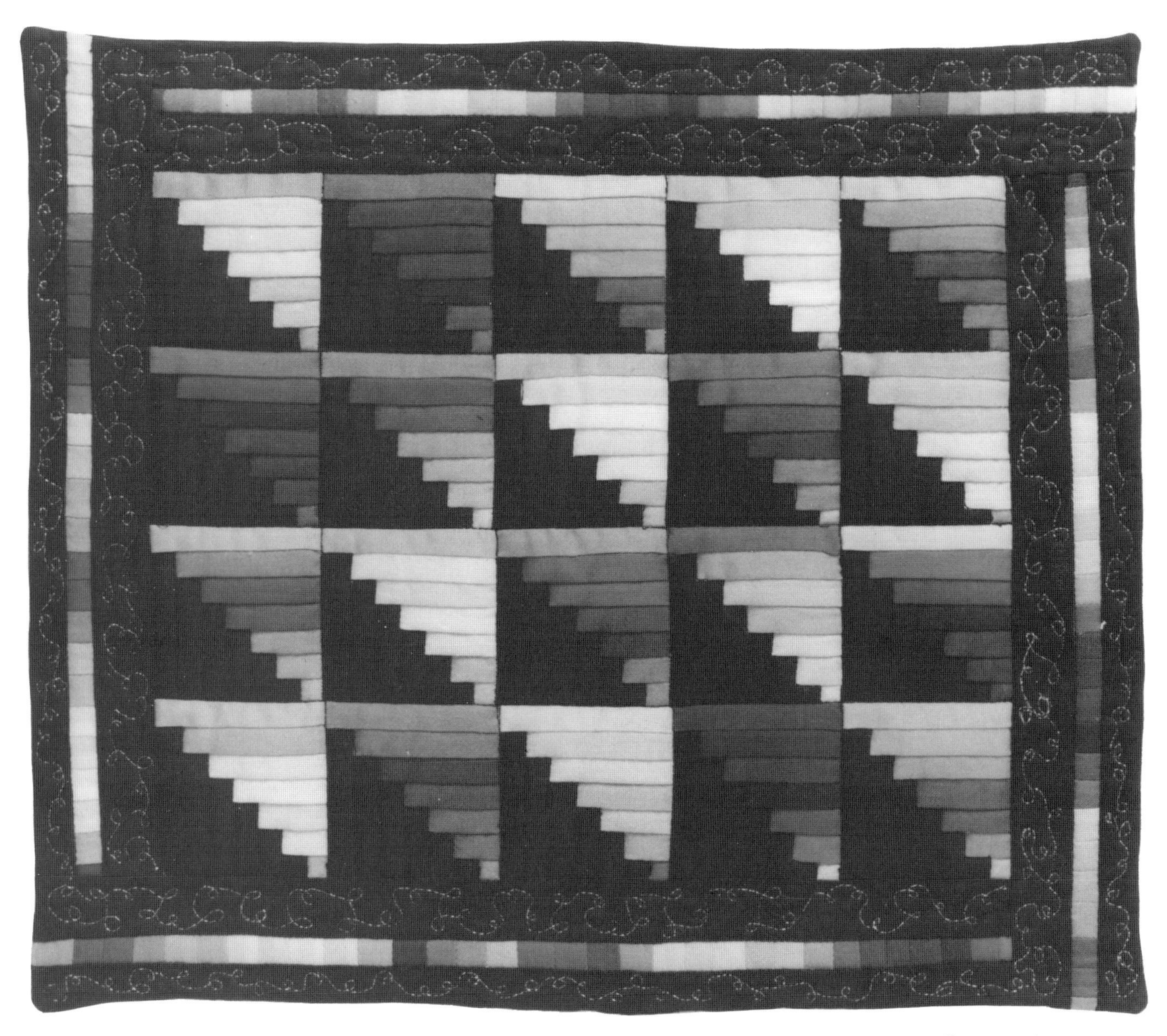

Shown in color on page 33

Special Techniques:

Strip Pieced Border
"No inset" Inset Piecing
Envelope Finish

Finished Quilt Size:

12 3/4" by 10 3/4""

Block Size:

2" square

I have a confession to make—this quilt made itself! Sometimes that happens. You start to make a quilt and it simply takes over—the fabrics are perfect, the pieces go together without a problem, you know exactly how many blocks to make and where to put them, the borders fit perfectly! A dear friend of mine, Kathy DeYoung, decided to make a color wheel quilt several years ago and dyed some fabrics herself and bought others. She made her quilt and took the leftover fabrics and cut them into 3" squares and gave me a little plastic bag with 36 squares and said make a color wheel. I said "someday" and tossed the little plastic bag into my fabric cabinet and forgot about it. When I started to write this book, the little plastic bag fell out of the closet. So I tossed it back in. A week or so later it fell out of the closet again, and again I threw it back. About the fourth time it happened, I stopped and said to myself, "I do believe these fabrics are trying to tell me something!"

In spite of the fact that these blocks are only 2" square and have thirteen patches they are very easy to make! I used 35 solids plus black. If the thought of finding and coordinating 35 fabrics has you in a panic, read on before you turn the page.

Now you may have a bunch of solids lurking in your stash and you likely have a few friends who also have some solids. So tell every one to cut 5" or 6" squares of each color (the 3" squares that I used were not quite large enough and I had to cheat on the seam allowances!)—one square of each fabric for each participant. Now everyone prepares stacks of squares with one square of each color in each stack and trades with everyone else. Take all these squares and lay them out, sorting by color and within a color from light to dark. Do you have roughly the same number of squares in each color—yellows from pale to gold; oranges from salmon to dark orange; red from pink to dark burgundy; purple from lilac to deep blue purple; greens from lime to dark forest green; blue from light to dark? You need several shades of each color ranging from light to dark. Perhaps you only need to find three or four fabrics to fill in the spaces.

No solids in your stash? Don't have anyone to trade with? If you look at the ads in the quilting magazines or in the mail order catalogues, you often see companies advertising packets of 3" or 4" squares for reasonable prices. On the other hand, there is nothing magic about using 35 fabrics, you can use more fabrics or fewer. And of course you can certainly use prints. I just took advantage of the fact that some one else had done all the work in collecting these fabrics.

The sense of movement in this quilt comes from both the use of many colors and the fact that the fabrics shade from light to dark to light, **Fig 1**. I laid out the yellows from darkest (gold) to lightest (pale yellow) and then decided that the palest green looked good next to the light yellow. So then I laid out the greens from light to dark after the yellows. The darkest blue came next shading down to the lightest blue. Then the purples/violets from light to dark and so on. I kept the fabrics in order while making the quilt and simply used whatever fabric was next for the next log.

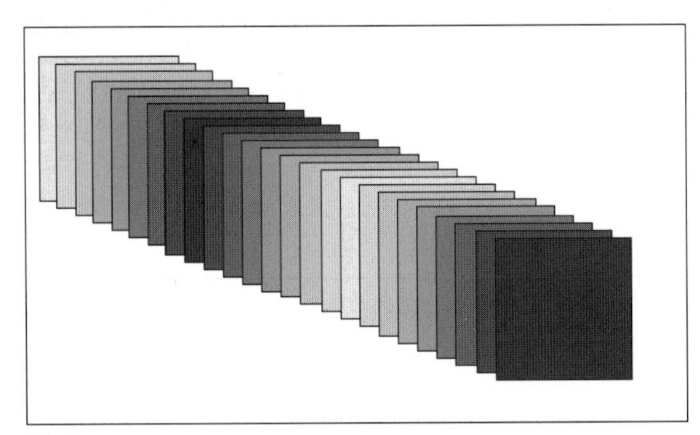

Fig 1

For the first set of ten blocks, make five blocks using seven different fabrics per block. Then, make five more blocks starting from the other end of the stack. For the second set of ten blocks, take the first fabric (gold) and move it to the end of the stack; continue in the same manner as above. No two blocks are alike, but the color flow is consistent. This is really a lot more fun to do than to read about!

Prepare twenty bases by your chosen method.

Supplies for Birds of a Feather Chevron (all fabric requirements are approximate)	
Black fabric	1/4 yd (includes border)
Bright fabric	about 1/4 yd total of assorted bright scraps (includes border)

Notes:

1. After you have arranged your bright scraps in a pleasing order, you may want to cut a tiny piece of each and glue them down onto a piece of paper in your chosen order. Family, friends, pets and mysterious strangers seem to sneak into my sewing room and rearrange things when my back is turned.

2. The finished size of the strips in these blocks is just over 1/4". If you want to precut some of your scraps, cut them a generous 3/4" wide. You will find it easier to roughly cut your log lengths as you get ready to add each log.

3. Make a sample block before you cut up all your fabric.

Assembly Directions

1. Cut a square of your first colored fabric about 3/4" by 3/4". This will be generously larger than you need, but if you cut your pieces smaller they are hard to work with. With the printed side of the base facing you, place a small dab of glue stick on the unprinted side in the middle of patch #1. Center your fabric right side up on the unprinted side of the base making sure that you have a seam allowance all around. The glue stick will keep the fabric from shifting.

2. With the printed side of the base towards you, fold the base toward you on the printed line between patch #1 and #2 (or a very scant 1/4" above the printed line if you are machine sewing) and pre-trim the raw edge of the fabric to a scant 1/4", being careful not to cut the base or move the patch. On blocks this small, your seam allowances should be a scant 1/4", but more than 1/8".

3. Following the numbers on the base, place second colored fabric face down on center patch, making sure that raw edge aligns with pre-trimmed edge of first patch, **Fig 2**. Hold base to light to make sure that patch overlaps edges of previous patch, leaving a seam allowance on all sides.

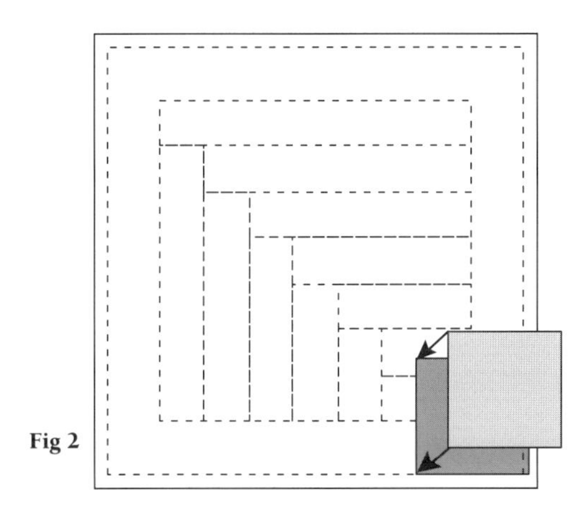

Fig 2

Sew on line between #1 and #2. Smooth log open; finger press or gently iron.

4. Fold base towards you on line between #2 and #3 (or a scant 1/4" above line), pre-trim and place a black log with raw edges aligned. Keep adding logs following the numbers. You will be alternating black logs and colored logs. Remember—pre-trim, align, sew, smooth open.

5. Make twenty blocks. Trim outside of blocks to a 1/4" seam allowance.

6. Lay out blocks in four rows of five blocks. Play with the color arrangement until you are happy with the movement of the colors across the surface of the quilt. Sew blocks together.

I.D.—*I have found that sometimes if a quilt arrangement just doesn't seem right, it may be because the quilt is upside down or sideways! On blocks such as the chevron, there is no real up or down. Your quilt may demand to be a long rectangle instead of a wide rectangle! If it demands to be square, you are just going to have to break down and make more blocks.*

Strip Pieced Border

1. To make border, cut eight strips of black fabric about 10" long and 1 1/4" wide. Cut strips of each colored fabric, 3/4" wide and 4" long, keeping colored strips in the same order as used for the blocks. Sew the strips into sets of seven fabrics using a scant 1/4" seam allowance; press all the seam allowances in the same direction. (I kept the sets at seven fabrics to minimize any stretching or warping of these little strips and to be able to play with the color arrangement in the borders). Cross cut each set every 3/4", **Fig 3**. You will have more colored strips than you will need.

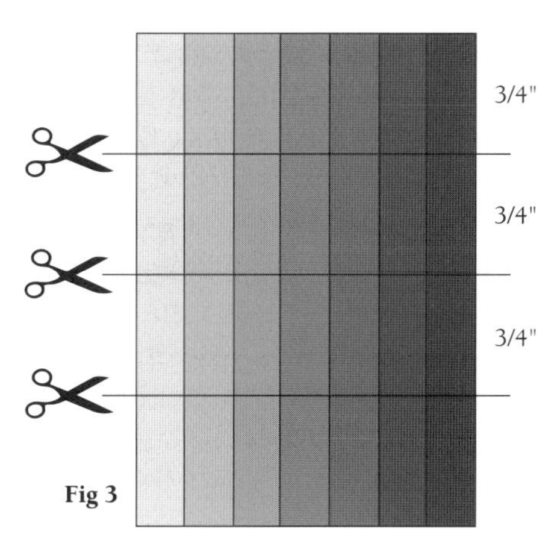

Fig 3

2. Lay a strip of black fabric on each side of the quilt. Do not sew them on. Lay your little colored strips next to the black strip, rearranging them until you have a pleasant arrangement, **Fig 4**. You may choose to have the colors the same in all four borders or you may opt to have the borders echo the colors of the blocks along the borders—there is no right or wrong arrangement.

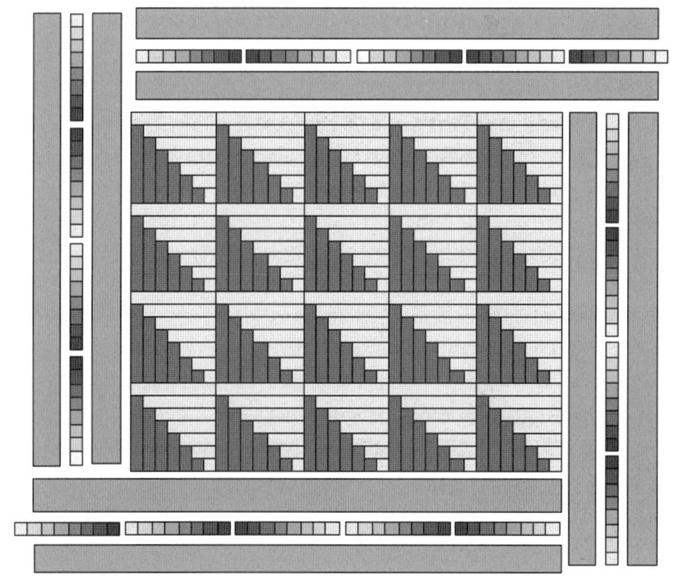

Fig 4

3. **Assembling the border:** Starting with one side of the quilt, sew the colored strips together end to end to form a long strip of little multi-colored blocks. Sew a black strip on each long side of the multi-colored strip. Repeat for all four borders.

"No inset" Inset Piecing for Border

1. If you studied the borders in the photograph at the beginning of this section, you may have noticed that each of the borders overlaps the next border and decided that this was either impossible to do or that you would have to somehow insert the quilt into the middle. There **is** a trick to doing this! Starting with any side, place one assembled border face up on the table. Place the quilt top face down on the border strip about 2 1/2" from the top of the border strip. Start sewing the quilt to the border about 1" below the top of the quilt and sew down to the bottom of the quilt, **Fig 5**.

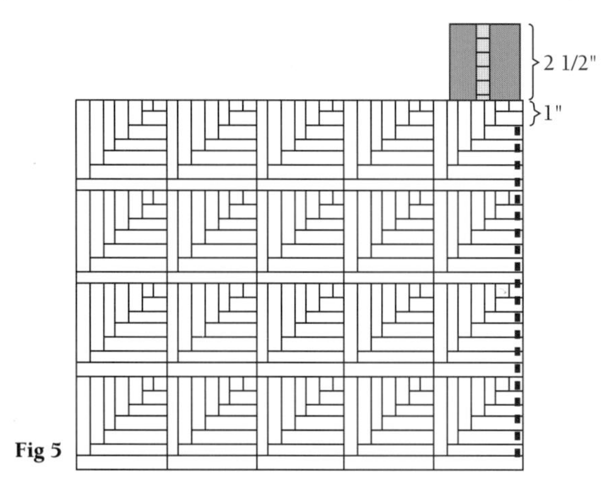

Fig 5

Turn quilt right side up, smooth open the border and press gently, pressing the seam allowance towards the border. Cut only the **bottom** of the border even with the quilt.

2. Place next strip face up on the table; turn quilt a quarter turn (first sewn border strip will be on upper edge) and place the quilt face down on the border strip. The previously sewn border should lay on top of the border strip, **Fig 6**. Sew from the top to the bottom. Smooth open and press as before, cutting the newly added strip even with lower edge of quilt. Add the third border in same manner. Add fourth border, making sure first border is folded out of the way so that it doesn't get caught in your stitching. Smooth open and press; cut strip even with lower edge.

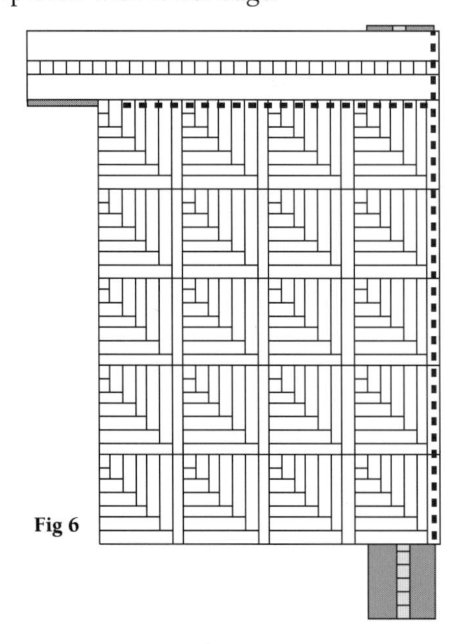

Fig 6

Remember that part of the first border that we didn't sew? Place first border strip over the fourth border and sew it down over the edge of the 4th border, **Fig 7**, and voila! No inset piecing!

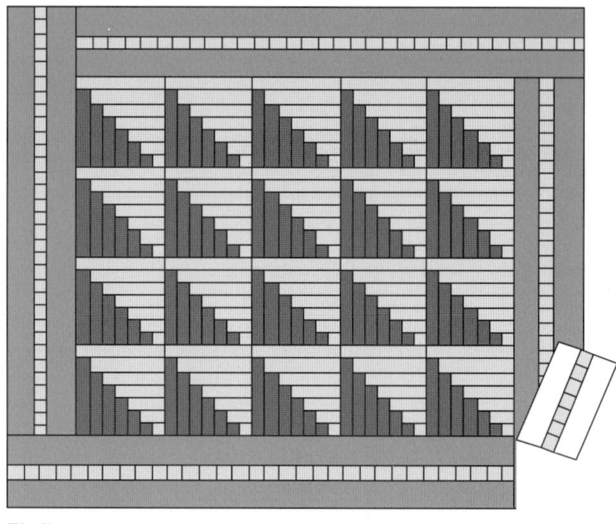

Fig 7

Envelope Finish

1. I decided to not use a binding on this quilt, but rather an envelope finish. Measure quilt top carefully and cut a piece of backing and a piece of batting about 1" larger in each direction. Lay batting on the table. Lay backing face up on batting. Place quilt top face down and centered on batting and backing.

2. Pin carefully, placing pins perpendicular to the quilt edges. Sew with 1/4" seam allowance leaving an opening for turning, **Fig 8**. To get square corners, sew around corner in a slight curve with very small stitches. (I cannot explain why sewing the corners in a curve makes the corners nice and square when the piece is turned, it just does). Trim backing and batting even with quilt top. Trim a little batting from the corners if they appear thick—do not trim backing and top. Turn quilt right side out, carefully pushing corners out. Turn in raw edges of opening and invisibly whip stitch closed by hand. Press edges carefully making sure that seam lies exactly on edge.

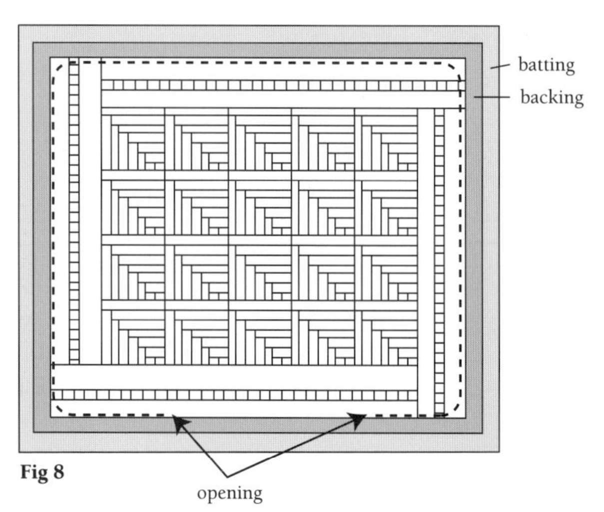

Fig 8

14. The photographed quilt was quilted in the ditch between each block and on each side of the multi-colored strips in the border. This quilt is so small and there are so many seam allowances that I think it would be impossible to hand quilt.

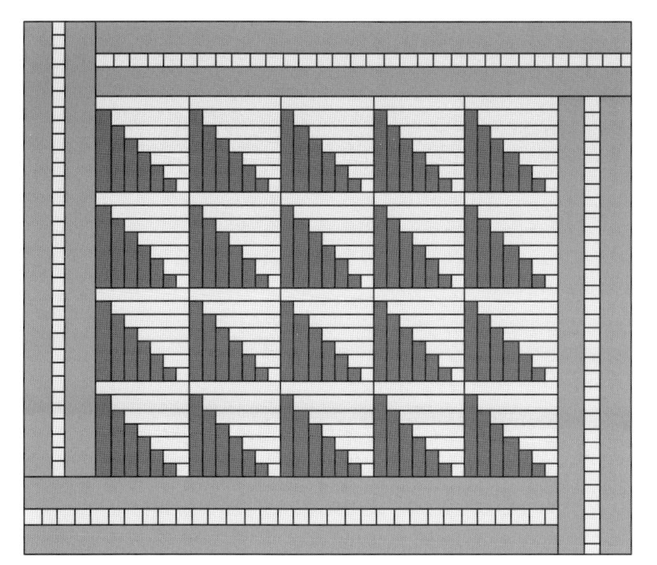

Quilt Layout

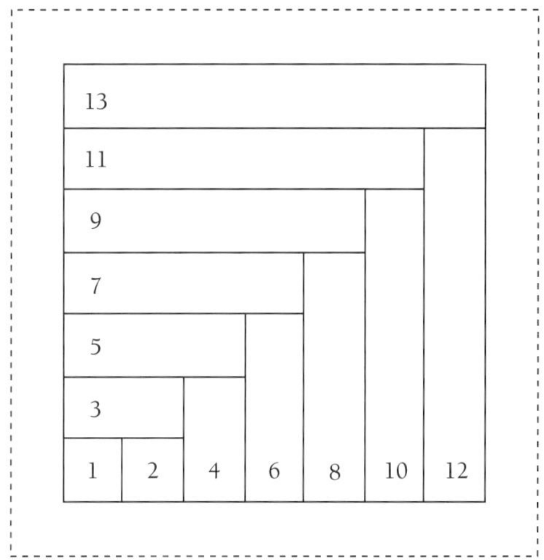

Chevron Quilt Block

Coloring Diagram

Pinwheels in the Garden - Wheel Block

Shown in color on page 34

Special Techniques:

Using Subunits
Setting Triangles
Modifying a Base

Quilt Size:

15" by 15"

Subunit size:

2" square

Block Size:

4" square

There are so many wonderful things that you can do with the Wheel subunit! When they are assembled as they are in this quilt, the blocks look as if they have been sashed. In Tornado, the medallion sampler quilt (page 54), the subunits are turned in a different direction before being assembled and look, to me, like the bow and ribbons on the top of a gift box. Also in the sampler, these subunits were used as the corners of the center Star block.

In this green and pink mini quilt, I turned the blocks on point, constructed a pieced border that "completed" the pinwheel sashing and added setting triangles and a binding. The subunit, **Fig 1**, has only four patches in it! The patches are numbered 1 through 4.

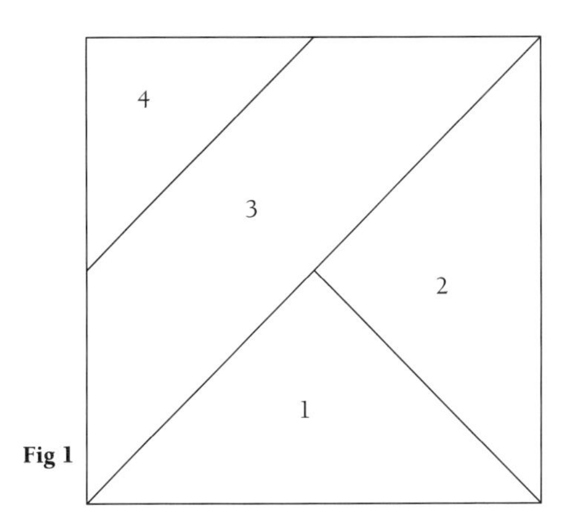

Fig 1

Now we really have to talk about mirror images again! Remember I said that the block that results from your piecing is the mirror image of the printed side of the base? That means that if you place a green fabric in the 2 position on the base (right side triangle), when the unit is completed that fabric will be the triangle on the left. A picture is worth a thousand words and in the case of mirror images maybe 10,000 words, **Fig 2**.

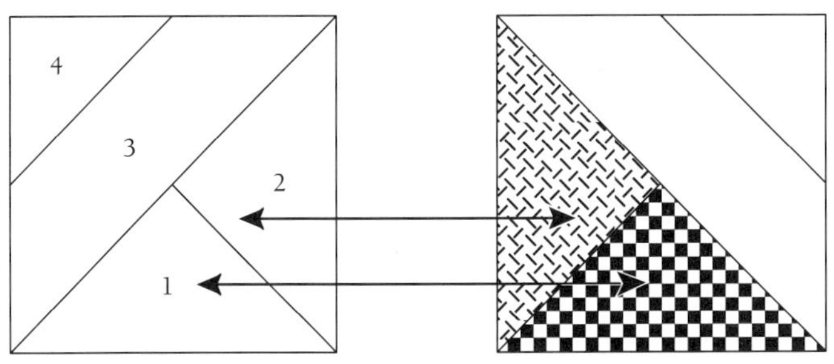

Fig 2

Here's the bottom line! If you are consistent in your fabric placement all your wheels will be turning in the same direction! If however you want all your wheels to turn clockwise (or counterclockwise), for example, here's what I do...trace the block onto thin paper with nice heavy lines including the letters and numbers. Turn the paper over and with colored pencils or markers color the unmarked side of the paper (or glue on scraps of fabric) so that it looks the way that you want the block to look. Turn the paper back over to the printed side and write yourself a little note: yellow print is fabric 2, green is fabric 1, etc. This is not cheating!

Let's reconstruct this quilt and see how it was made. The quilt consists of four Wheel blocks. Each Wheel block is four subunits. So you need sixteen copies of the subunit on either muslin or paper. The border, which completes the "sashing," uses eight more subunits (which are cut in half) along with some loose squares and rectangles of fabric.

Prepare 24 bases by your chosen method.

Supplies (all fabric requirements are approximate)	
fabric 1	1/8 yd or equivalent scraps
fabric 2	1/8 yd or equivalent scraps
fabric 3	1/8 yd or equivalent scraps
fabric 4	1/8 yd or equivalent scraps
Setting Triangles	two 10 1/2" squares cut along one diagonal

Notes:

1. Except for the yardage needed for the setting triangles, you can use small scraps for the rest of the quilt.

2. You can rough cut 2" squares for piece 1 and piece 2; 3 3/4" by 1 1/4" rectangles for piece 3 and 2 1/4" by 1 1/2" rectangles for piece 4. These are generous sizes but are big enough to ensure that you have seam allowances on all sides.

3. Make a sample before you cut up all your fabric.

Assembly Directions

1. With printed side of base facing you, place a small dab of glue stick on unprinted side in middle of patch #1. Center fabric 1 piece right side up on unprinted side of base making sure that you have seam allowance all around.

2. With printed side of base facing you, fold base toward you on line between #1 and #2 (or 1/4" above the line if you are machine stitching) and pre-trim to a scant 1/4" seam allowance.

3. Place fabric 2 patch face down on patch #1 with raw edges of #1 and #2 aligned on pre-trimmed edge of #1. Sew on line between #1 and #2, smooth patch open and finger press or gently iron.

4. Fold base toward you along line between #1#2 and #3; pre-trim raw edges to a scant 1/4" seam allowance. Place patch #3 face down aligning raw edges. Sew, smooth open the patch and press. Add patch #4.

5. Make sixteen of these units—four units are used for each block. Lay blocks out in a pleasing arrangement. Square up each unit leaving 1/4" seam allowance all around; sew units together. If you are sewing on paper bases, remove the paper in the seam allowances after sewing so that you can press the seam allowances nice and flat.

6. At this point, make the border shown in the photographed quilt or simply add plain sashing strips, **Fig 3**. If you wish to add plain sashing, cut two strips 2 1/2" by 8 1/2" long and two strips 2 1/2" by 10 1/2" long. Using a 1/4" seam allowance, sew the two shorter strips on two opposite sides of the quilt. Press seam allowances towards sash. Trim narrow ends of the just sewn-on borders even with the edges of the quilt if necessary. Sew on the other two strips.

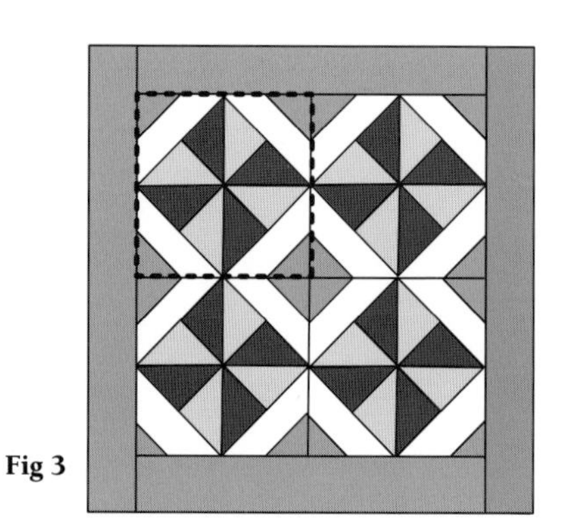

Fig 3

Piecing the Border

Modifying a Base

1. To make the pieced border, take the extra eight subunit bases and modify them as follows: Lay ruler along the base; draw a line across base through tip of piece #1, **Fig 4**. This will become the new edge of the unit.

2. Draw a second line 1/4" above the first line, **Fig 5**. Cut off remainder of base just outside second line. You should now have a unit that looks like a flying goose!

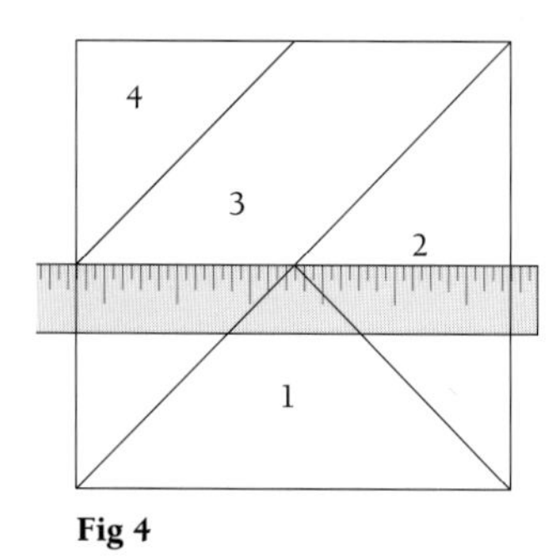

Fig 4

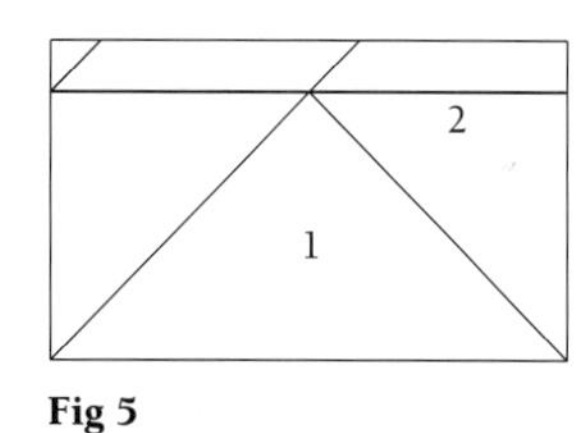

Fig 5

3. Place fabric 3 right side up on the wrong side of the base covering patch #1, pre-trim one edge and add patch #2 using fabric 4. Repeat for patch #3. Make eight of these units.

Adding the Borders

1. From fabric 4, cut eight rectangles 2 1/2" by 1 1/2" and four squares 1 1/2" by 1 1/2".

2. Lay out border pieces as shown in **Fig 6**; sew each border strip together. Sew assembled borders to quilt.

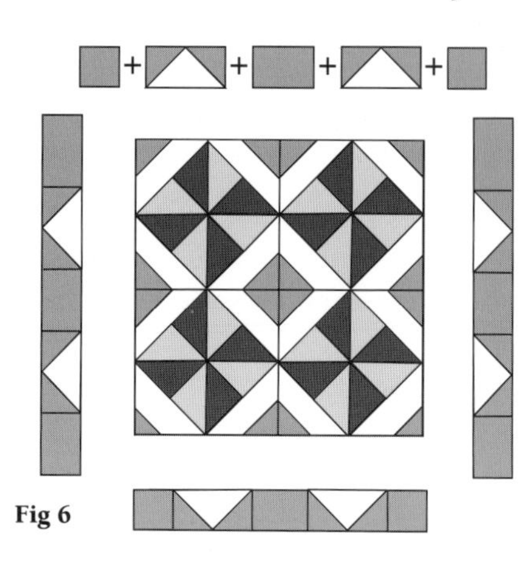

Fig 6

Adding Setting Triangles

Note: *The setting triangles at the corners have intentionally been cut larger than needed to "float" the center of the quilt. This means that the corners of the center of the quilt do not come all the way out to the edge.*

1. Take each setting triangle and find center of longest (diagonal) edge. Mark center with a pin. Find center of one edge of quilt. Lay quilt face down on setting triangle, aligning centers; pin together gently. Remember that this long edge of setting triangle is on the bias and will stretch and ripple if not handled carefully.

2. With setting triangle on bottom, sew edge of quilt and setting triangle together with 1/4" seam. ***Note:*** *The bias edge of triangle will be larger than side of the quilt.*

3. Sew a triangle to opposite edge of quilt. Open both setting triangles; press seams towards triangles.

4. Place a triangle (matching centers as above) on third side of the quilt. (Notice that edge overlaps the previous triangles.) Sew with 1/4" seam allowance from edge to edge.

5. Add fourth triangle. Press third and fourth triangles open, trimming out excess fabric to 1/4", **Fig 7**.

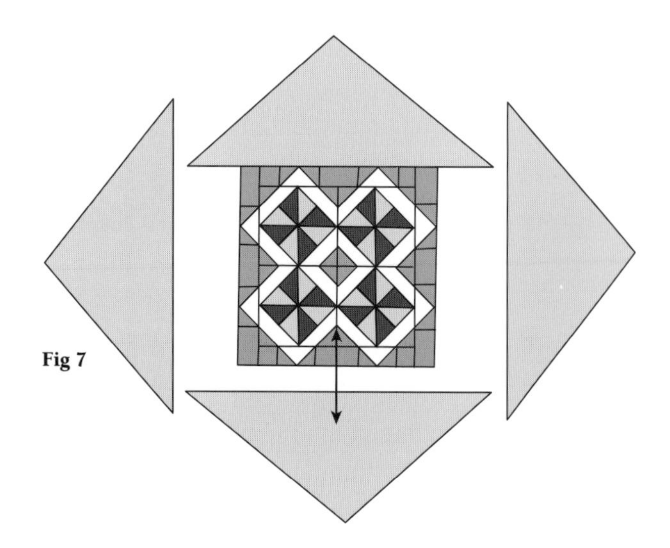

Fig 7

6. Square up quilt carefully, leaving equal amounts of "float" on all four sides. If you don't want quilt to float, then square up leaving exactly 1/4" seam allowance all around. Sometimes you aren't sure whether or not you want to float the center—what I do is to use these larger triangles as we did here and then cut them down as necessary.

I.D.—*Do **not** read this if you hated math in school! Did you ever wonder how to figure out the size of the triangles necessary to put a block on point? Or wonder what size a block would be after it is put on point? Well, if you remember math class, the teacher talked about* $a^2 + b^2 = c^2$ *where a and b were the sides of a square or rectangle and c was the diagonal (or hypotenuse) and that if you knew two of the values, you could solve for the third? Don't remember that? Well neither does anyone else. The important thing to remember is that if you know the length of the **side** of a square or half square triangle and you want to know the length of the diagonal, multiply by 1.414. If you happen to know the length of the diagonal, but not the length of the side, divide by 1.414. I find it real convenient that the standard seam allowance in quilting is 1/4" and that this number is 1.414. I just keep saying to myself, "1 4 1 4 1 4..." Anyway, if you use this method just round up the result to the nearest inch for a good approximation.*

Finishing the Quilt

The photographed quilt was machine quilted, but the big triangles would be a great place to do some hand quilting! The #1 and #4 fabric areas were stipple quilted to give added dimension to the pinwheels. See Finishing Up, pages 59 and 60, for directions on binding.

Here is a coloring diagram for you to play with. This block has great possibilities for some interesting quilts!

Quilt Layout

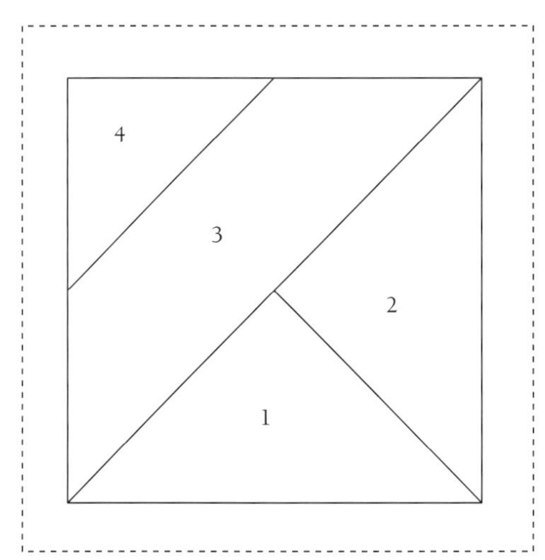

Pinwheel Quilt Block

Coloring Diagram

Snail's Trail

Shown in color on page 36

Special Techniques:
The "Impossible" Seam

Quilt Size:
16" by 16"

Block Size:
4" square

The Snail's Trail is one of those wonderful old patterns that quilters never tire of making. I decided to make my quilt mostly in black and white after I had to make a block for a swap. My friend Patsy Eckman turned her blocks and set them in the variation called Virginia Reel, page 29.

The Snail's Trail is a nonsymmetric block, so we have to stop and remember that the actual block will be the mirror image of the pattern that you see on the printed side of the base. Again, the important thing is to be consistent! If you make each foundation the same way and add the fabrics in the same order, the blocks will all spin in the same direction. (See the discussion of mirror images in the "Getting Started," page 5).

On the block diagram, **Fig 1**, notice that each patch has a number and a letter. Each patch is either A, B, C or D plus a number—that's just to help you remember which patches are what color. So decide on your colors or sort your scraps into darks and lights. Now write yourself a note, A's are __________, B's are __________, C's are ____________, and D's are _________. (I'm a big believer in notes!)

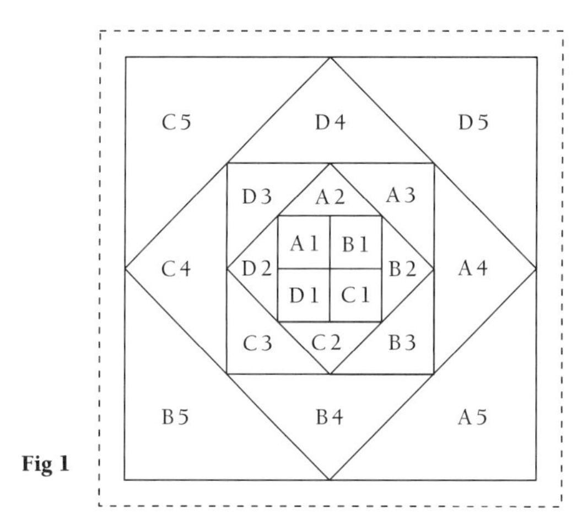

Fig 1

The Impossible Seam

This block also introduces the "impossible seam." When you piece on a base, the patch that you are about to add must completely cover the raw edge of the previous patch or patches. If it doesn't, then you have a seam that can't be sewn except by special techniques. If you study the center of this block, you notice that it is a four-patch. Let's think this through. Place one little square face up; pre-trim. Put the second piece face down, raw edges aligned; sew. Smooth open and place the third little square; sew and smooth. So far, so good. But, when we get to the fourth little square, if we sew the raw edge to the third square then we have an unsewn seam between 2 and 4, **Fig 2**, and if we sew the 4th square to the 2nd then it's open between 3 and 4!

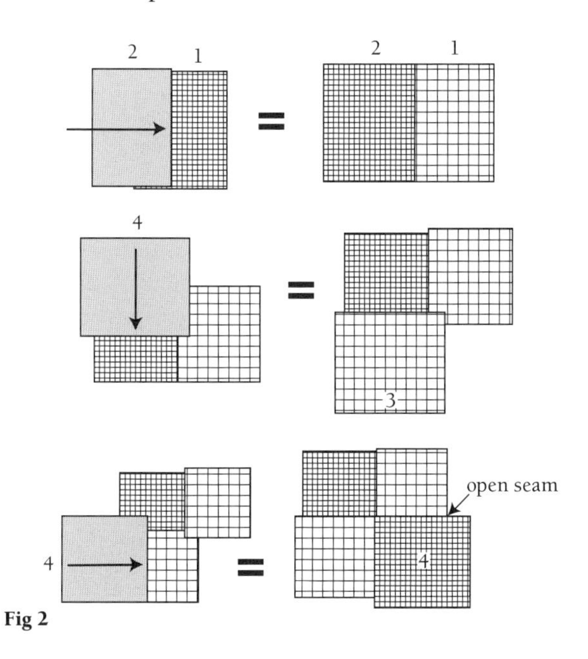

Fig 2

There are several ways, in general, to deal with this "challenge." Pre-sew the seam before starting to sew and treat the two patches as a single unit or fold under the seam allowance and hand sew the seam with an applique stitch; or visually create a seam that doesn't exist (which is what we did with the House block). In the case of the Snail's Trail, the easiest solution is to pre-sew sets of two little squares in advance. Now I know that you are looking at this block and feeling depressed at the thought of cutting out itty bitty squares and trying to sew them together, so that is **not** what we are going to do. What we are going to do is to take two strips of fabric wide enough to feel comfortable with, sew them together and then subcut them. When we pre-trim, the excess fabric will be cut off. Again we waste a little bit of fabric but we work with pieces large enough to handle easily.

The photographed quilt, page 36, uses two colors (white and black/white prints) while the Snail block in the sampler uses three colors (front cover). You may chose to do a two-, three- or four-color Snail's Trail blocks. If you are doing a two-color Snail, then fabric A and C are one color or color family and fabrics B and D are a second color; a three-color Snail **(Fig 1)** would have one color for patches marked A, one color for patches marked C and a third color for patches marked B and D. I find it helpful to either mark the colors on the base or make myself a little "cheat sheet" with scraps of fabric or colored pencils.

Prepare nine muslin or paper bases by your chosen method.

Supplies (all fabric requirements are approximate)	
A fabric	1/4 yd of dk print fabric or an equivalent amount of scraps
B fabric	1/4 yd of lt print fabric or an equivalent amount of scraps
C fabric	1/4 yd of dk print fabric or an equivalent amount of scraps
D fabric	1/4 yd of lt print fabric or an equivalent amount of scraps
Flap fabric	four strips of fabric 3/4" wide and about 13 1/2" long
Border fabric	two strips, 2" by 13" and two strips, 2" by 17" or more if a wider border is desired

Notes:

1. The center four-patch is made by sewing strips of fabrics A and B together which are 1 1/4" wide and about 12" long. The sewn set is then crosscut every 1 1/4", **Fig 3**. If using scraps, simply sew as many pieces together as needed to get nine pre-sewn side-by-side squares. Repeat using fabric C and D strips. You will need nine side-by-side squares from each set (eighteen total).

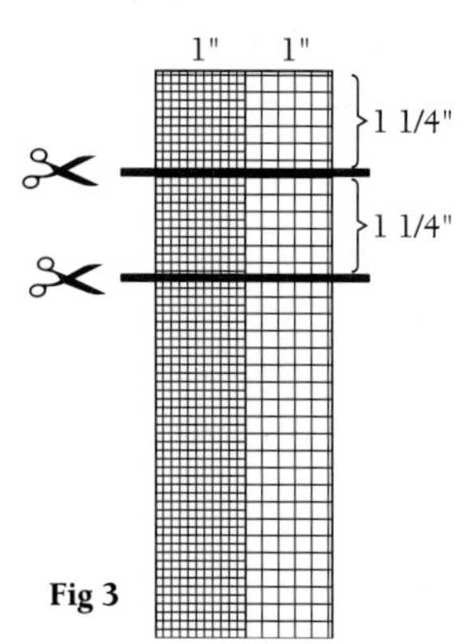

Fig 3

2. I found it easiest to use rough-cut rectangles instead of triangles when piecing this block (which should not stop you from experimenting with rough-cut triangles to see if you are comfortable with them). The smallest triangles need rough-cut rectangles about 1 1/4" by 1 1/4", the next size triangles need 1 3/4" by 1 1/2", the next 2 3/4" by 1 1/2", and the largest 3 1/2" by 1 3/4". This does waste some fabric but it also keeps you from attaching a piece that is too small (and then having to rip it out). Don't get too obsessive here about cutting these rectangles—I usually cut some little rectangles and some big ones (a bunch that are 3 1/2" by 1 3/4" and a bunch that are 2 3/4" by 1 1/2"). I then use the smaller ones for the two smaller size triangles and the larger ones for the two larger size triangles. The 1/4 yd of each fabric called for in the supplies is more than enough!

3. Make a sample before you cut up all your fabric.

Assembly Directions

1. Make eighteen sets (nine of each) of side-by-side squares as described above. If you find it difficult to handle strips this narrow, use wider strips—the excess fabric will disappear in the assembly process. You can also crosscut at wider intervals. Adjust your fabric requirements upwards if you do this, but still use a 1/4" seam allowance.

2. Put a small dab of glue stick on unprinted side of base. Hold base up to the light, printed side towards you and place pre-sewn squares right side up on unprinted side making sure that sewn seam lies directly over line between patches A1 and B1, **Fig 4**; leave enough fabric to overlap the printed lines for seam allowances. This placement takes a little fooling around to get perfect, but don't get frustrated! It's worth the effort (and anyway you are only going to do it eight more times!) I find that if I mark the center and cross lines on the unprinted side and extend them a little, it helps me to line these up.

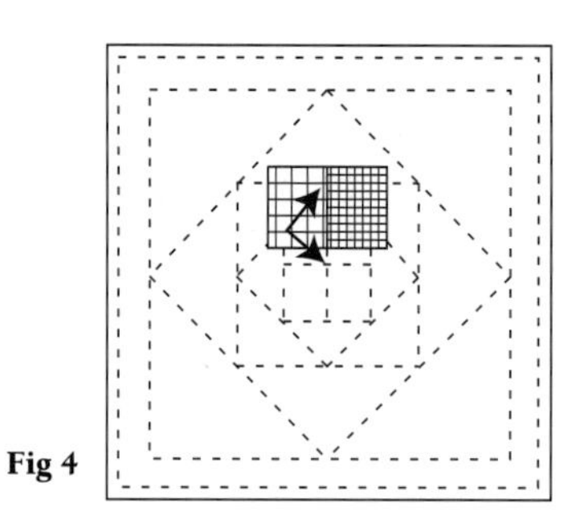
Fig 4

3. With printed side of base towards you, fold on printed line between A1B1 and D1C1 (or 1/4" above the line if you are machine sewing) and pre-trim, being careful not to move the patch.

4. Place another set of pre-sewn squares (so that the D fabric lies on the A fabric and C on B) face down on first set making sure that pre-sewn seams are perfectly aligned and that raw edges align, **Fig 5**. Sew on line between A1B1 and D1C1. Smooth patch open; finger press or gently iron.

5. Continue folding base, pre-trimming and adding patches following numbers and letters, **Fig 6**.

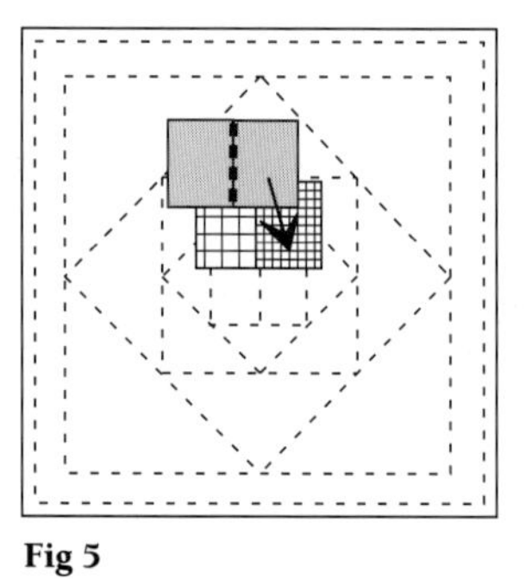
Fig 5

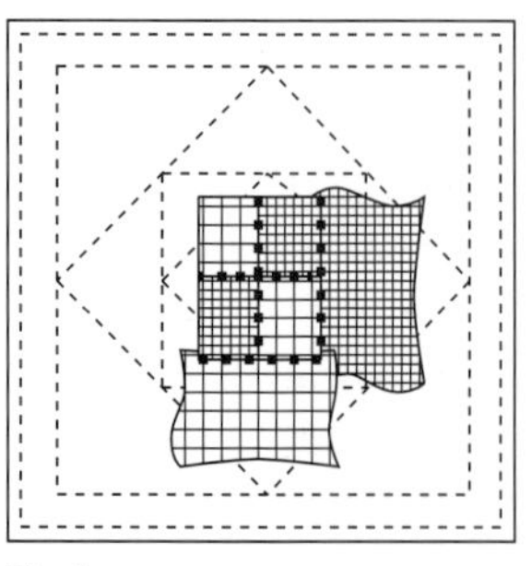
Fig 6

6. Make nine blocks and lay them out in a pleasing arrangement. Square up each block leaving a 1/4" seam allowance; sew the blocks together.

7. To make the border fabric "go with" the Snail's Trail blocks, I decided that I needed a flap between the blocks and the border. This is nothing more than a very narrow strip of fabric with a folded edge—think of it as similar to the corded insertion that you see on couch pillows without the cording. Flaps add visual interest and dimensionality to a quilt.

To make a flap, measure edge of piece—yours should be about 12 1/2" including seam allowance. Cut four 3/4"-wide by 13 1/2"-long strips of fabric. Fold fabric lengthwise with **wrong sides together**; press gently. Lay quilt right side up; place flap along one edge with raw edges of the quilt and flap even. Using a regular stitch length, slowly and carefully sew flap to quilt edge with a 1/8" seam allowance, **Fig 6**. Sew a flap to opposite side of quilt; trim ends of strips even with quilt. Sew flaps on remaining two sides and trim.

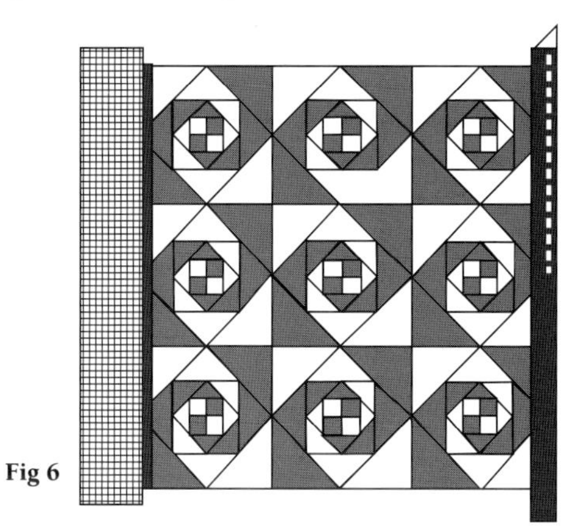
Fig 6

Hint: *If you can adjust the needle position on your machine, try adjusting the needle one or two places to the right and keep the edge of the flap lined up at your usual 1/4" seam allowance mark. Remember to put your needle back to its center or standard position when you are done!*

Practice sewing flap on some scraps of fabric if you have never done one before. It is a technique that requires a lot of precision but it's worth learning.

R.R.R.—*No one will know that you had to "practice," but they will if you don't.*

8. Place first (shorter) border piece right side up on a flat surface. Starting on the side of the quilt where you attached the first flap, lay quilt face down on border, raw edges aligned. (You should now be able to see the line of stitching where you attached the flap.) Sew border to quilt with a 1/4" seam allowance making sure that you are sewing a consistent distance to the left of the flap stitching line. Add border to opposite side of quilt; press borders open. Sew borders on remaining two sides. Remember the last two border pieces must be long enough to extend over the first two borders!

9. Photographed model was "echo" quilted in the light snails—I used several lines of stitching about 1/4" apart following the curve of the white patches. See Finishing Up, pages 59 and 60, for binding directions.

Quilt Layout

- Make sure that all your bases look the same before you start and that you know where the dark and light fabrics will be placed.
- Pre-sew squares for center.
- Make sure that the pre-sewn seams are lined up with the lines on the base.
- Did you notice the misplaced dark in the center block of my quilt? I didn't until it was assembled and the borders were on!

Alternate View:

Quilt Size:

15 3/4" by 15 3/4"

Patsy Eckman used only four Snail's Trail blocks in holiday colors to make a wonderful Christmas wallhanging. By creatively using four borders, she made a little bit of piecing into a whole lot of quilt! She framed the four blocks with a 1/4" (cut 3/4") strip of black, then a 2" (cut 2 1/2") border of a light fabric, another 1/4" black border and a final 2" border of a medium/large poinsettia print to tie it all together. For added interest and dimension, she glued some little red sequin stars here and there on the wide light border!

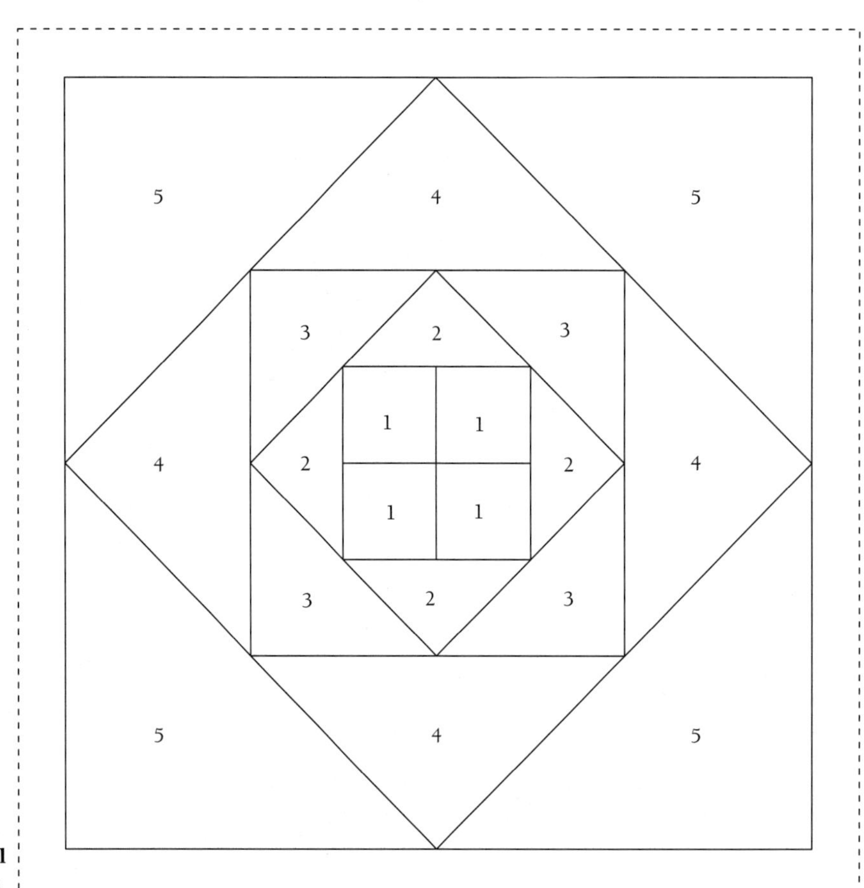

Snail's Trail Quilt Block

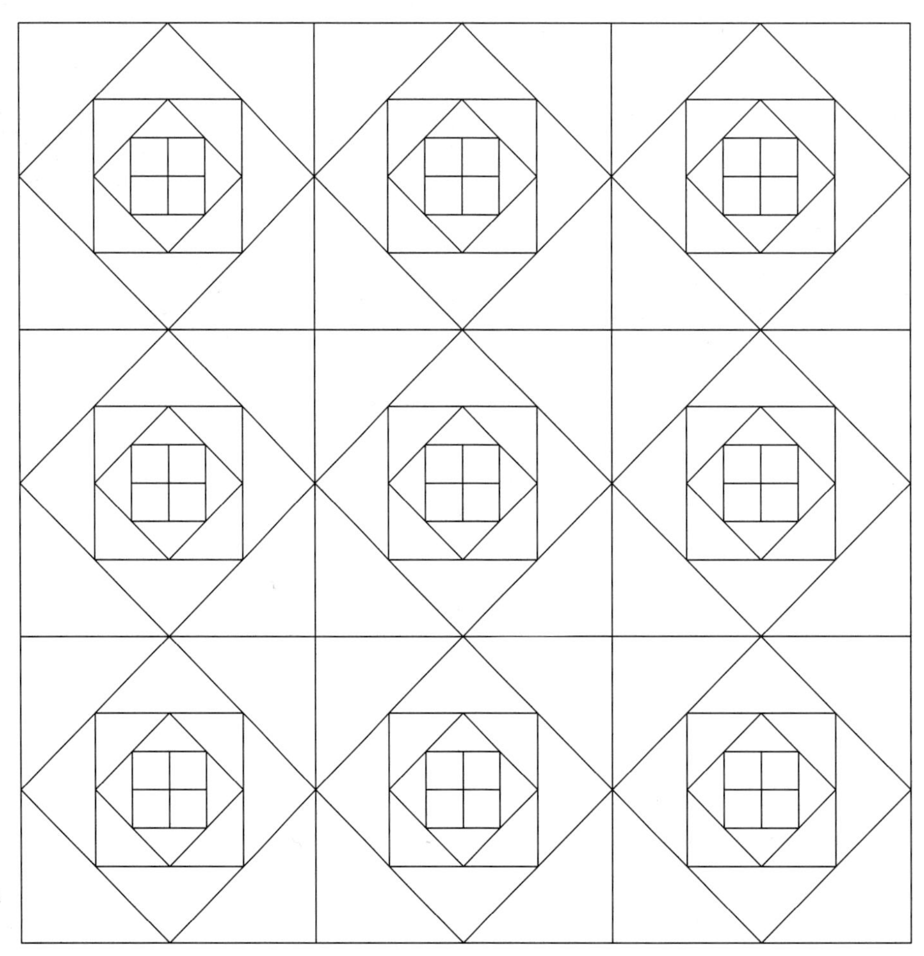

Coloring Diagram

Pineapple

Shown in color on back cover

Special Technique:
Faux Binding

Quilt Size:
10 1/4" by 10 1/4"

Block Size:
4" square

The Pineapple block is classified as a Log Cabin variation because of the similarities of having a square in the center and logs that encircle it. To me, the Pineapple is a completely different challenge to both draft and color! While the Log Cabin gives you four quadrants to color, the Pineapple has eight! Every time I try to make Pineapple blocks without sitting down and coloring them first, I am always surprised at the results—sometimes happily, sometimes not. This is a (positive) challenge not a (negative) problem. The possibilities are wonderful!

As you saw in the "Birds of a Feather" quilt (page XX), using black as a background color makes your colors glow. White is also a wonderful background or contrast color. I managed to sneak in one of my favorite fabrics - the little black and white check. The fabric that I used to "coordinate" the colors for this quilt doesn't appear anywhere in the quilt—after I chose all the fabrics, the original fabric no longer "worked." By the way, this happens frequently in quiltmaking! Just take that wonderful fabric that got you started, thank it nicely for helping you design your quilt and put it carefully in your fabric stash for another day.

As I chose the fabrics for this quilt, I tried to select fabrics that didn't contrast too much with each other within each color group, because I wanted the colors to make the statement. Most of these fabrics are "tone on tone" or monochromatic prints—single color prints with either a small design in black or another shade of the same color. This type of print gives a lot of depth to your quilt, but "reads" as a solid or single color fabric. You could of course use closely shaded solid color fabrics instead of prints.

This block is actually rather easy to piece—a square in the center, four little triangles around it and then a series of logs. Do not be daunted because it has 49 pieces. The last four pieces are triangles which make the block square! Yes they really are square! Because the borders and the four corner triangles are black and because they are quilted as if they were one patch, at first glance it looks as if the block is octagonal.

Prepare four bases by your chosen method.

Supplies (all fabric requirements are approximate)	
Bright colors	scraps of yellow, blue, pink and purple fabrics (the equivalent of 1" by 44" strip of each color)
Black fabric	1/4 yd (includes border)
White fabric	1/8 yd
Faux binding and backing	11" x 15" piece
Center squares	scrap of checkered fabric

Notes:

1. Lay a piece of tracing paper over the coloring diagram at the end of this section and play around with color combinations. What happens if you place the bright colors on the diagonal logs and the black and white on the horizontal and verticals?

2. The numbering on this block is a little different from the other blocks—instead of numbering each patch, I numbered each "round." So the center is C and the first round (the little triangles) are all numbered 1; the next round (the first of the logs) are all 2, etc. It doesn't matter which triangle you start with in round 1 or which log you start with in round 2 as long as you do the rounds in numerical order.

3. In order to keep fabric placements correct, label each patch on the base with a color code—P for purple; B for blue, Y for yellow, R for pink (red), W for white and nothing for black, **Fig 1**. Mark all four bases exactly the same way.

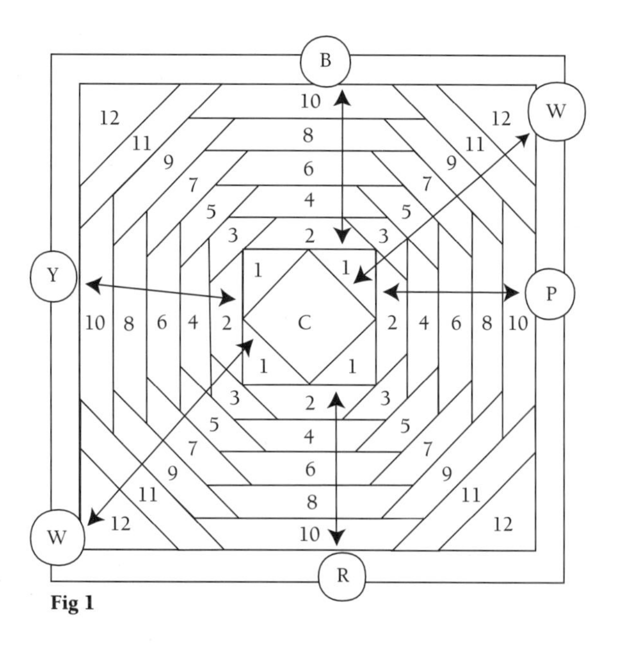

Fig 1

4. Make a sample before you cut up all your fabric.

Assembly Directions

1. Put a small dab of glue stick on the unprinted side of the base in the center of the C patch. Cut a center square about 1 1/4" by 1 1/4" and place it face up on the unmarked side of the base making sure that you have seam allowances on all sides. With printed side of base facing you, fold base on line (or 1/4" above the line if you are machine sewing) between C and one of the #1 triangle spaces; pre-trim raw edge to a scant 1/4".

2. Rough-cut a 1 1/4" square of white fabric and place it face down over C with the raw edges aligned. Sew on line between C and 1. Smooth patch open; finger press or gently iron.

continued on page 37

Birds of a Feather Chevron

"Rain, Rain Go Away" Log Cabin

Pinwheels in the Garden

Bonus Blocks

Storm at Sea

Crazy Patch Houses

Tree Ornaments
Practice Block

Snail's Trail

Snail's Trail

3. Fold base towards you on line between C and next #1 triangle space; pre-trim. Rough-cut a 1 1/4" square of black, place it face down, align raw edges and sew. Smooth open. Continue in this manner for the next two triangle spaces, alternating black and white.

4. For the remaining piecing, you will be adding logs. You may find it easier to precut some logs about 1" by 2" for the next couple of rounds and 1" by 2 1/2" for the 3rd, 4th and 5th rounds. These log sizes are generous—it wastes a little fabric but it gives you pieces large enough to hold on to! Following your color code on the base, add one log of each color for round #2. (Remember—pre-trim, place log face down with raw edges aligned, sew, and smooth open).

5. Fold base towards you on line between #2 and #3, **Fig 2**.***Warning!*** It is very easy to accidentally fold on the line between #2 and #4 and chop off log #2! (Take it from one who knows!) So double check that you have folded on the right line before pre-trimming—you should see some of the colored fabrics from round #2 as well as the point from round 1 sticking up. Round #3 patches are the alternating black and white logs.

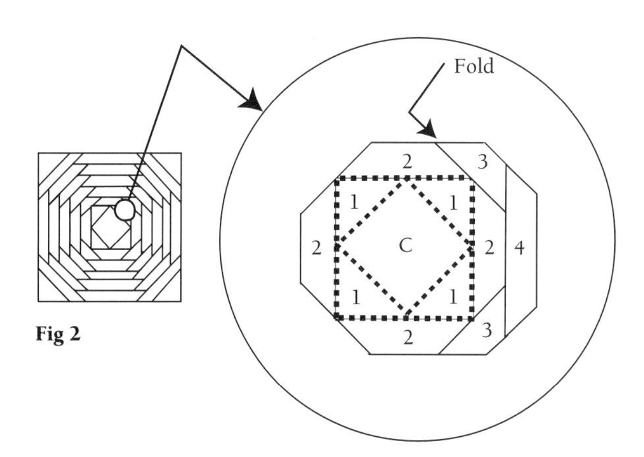

Fig 2

6. Continue adding logs until you get to round #11. Because of the color placement I chose, round #11 and round #12 are identical, so I took the lazy way and simply cut 2 1/2" squares of black and white fabrics, sewed on the lines between round #9 and round #11 and ignored round #12. If you have chosen a different coloration, simply add round #11 and then round #12.

7. After you have made four blocks, trim outside edges of blocks leaving 1/4" seam allowance. Lay your blocks out, twisting and turning them until you have a pleasing arrangement; sew blocks together.

8. Cut black strips for borders: two strips 1 1/2" by 8 1/2", two strips 1 1/2" by 10 1/2". Sew the two shorter borders to opposite sides of the quilt. Press open and add the two longer borders.

Finishing the Quilt

Faux Binding

1. For Faux Binding, cut four strips 3/4" wide by 10 3/4". (The fabric for these strips should be the same as your backing fabric.)

2. Attach two strips to opposite sides of quilt; trim top and bottom edges of border strip even with non-bordered edges of quilt.

3. Attach remaining two strips.

4. Layer batting, then backing (face up) and quilt top (face down) for an envelope finish; sew along all edges, leaving an opening for turning. (See Envelope Finish in "Birds in the Air," page 20, for detailed directions.)

5. Turn quilt right side out; hand stitch opening closed. Stitch "in the ditch" (exactly on the seam) between the black border and the faux binding. I want to thank Marti Michell for showing me this terrific way to make a quilt look like it has a binding when it doesn't!

Quilting

The photographed quilt was stipple quilted in the center and borders with a variegated rayon thread. I just love variegated threads! I quilted right over the black corner triangles on the blocks as I quilted the borders which makes the center of the quilt look octagonal.

- Make sure to mark your color placement on the bases before you start, it's easy to lose track of what comes next on this block.
- When adding rounds 3, 5, 7, 9 and 11, make sure you are pre-trimming correctly.

Quilt Layout

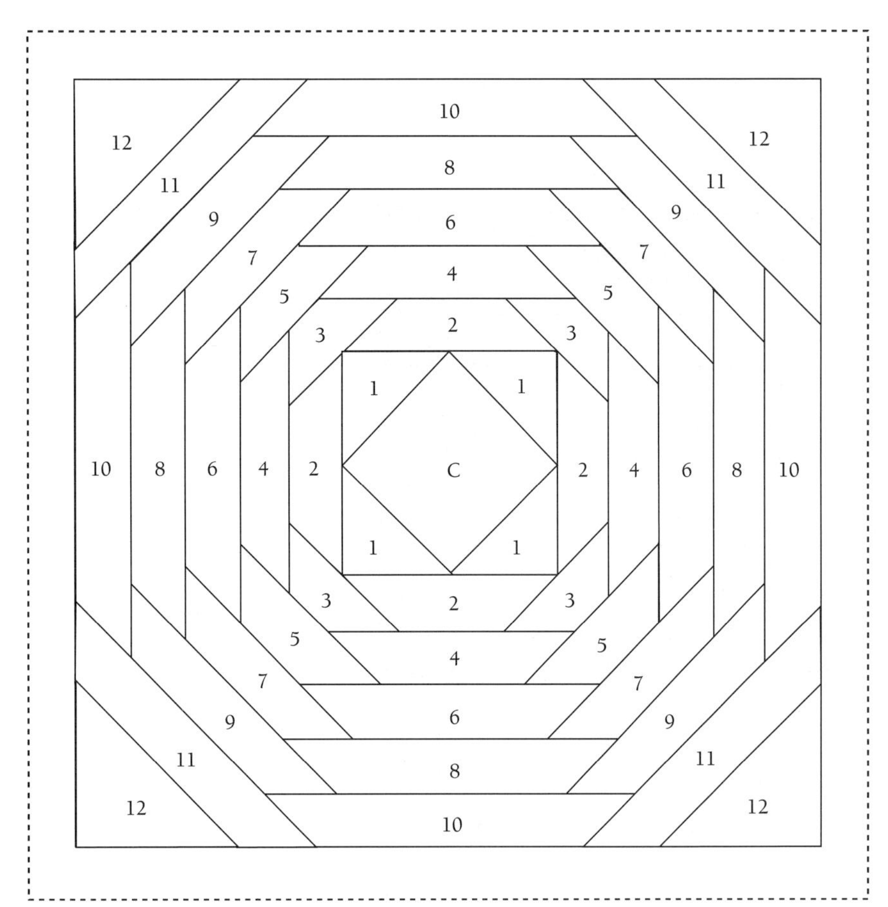

Pineapple Quilt Block

Coloring Diagram

Storm at Sea

Shown in color on page 34

Special Techniques:

Secondary Patterns
Mitered Borders

Quilt Size:

16 1/2" by 23 1/2"

Center Block Size:

4" square

Storm at Sea—a wonderful quilt pattern with a terrible name! The Storm at Sea is different from the other quilts that we are doing because it is not a single block which is then repeated to make the quilt but rather three distinct blocks - the Square in the Square center block and two blocks which form sashing around the center. Oh, the reason I hate the name—well, there are so many interesting secondary patterns that can be brought out by changing the color placement in your patches, **Fig 1**—hearts, stars, octagons as well as the diagonal waves that seem to move across the surface of the quilt.

This quilt pattern looks wonderful in all kinds of color schemes, not just blue and white! By the way, the star that appears where four blocks come together is the same star that is used as the center of the Medallion Sampler quilt (page 54).

Secondary Patterns

The different possibilities in this quilt are determined by placement of your darks and lights. In order to "pop" the hearts or the stars or the waves, you have to have contrast between the various patches. This is definitely a pattern where you should take the time to color or make a mock up of a few blocks before you start piecing, especially when you have a particular secondary pattern that you want to emphasize. If, however, you simply love all the variations of Storm at Sea and want to be surprised by how the fabrics work together, then separate your darks and your lights and start piecing. For the photographed quilt, I used four dark prints and two pink prints. One of the pink prints is actually a fabric with large pink, purple and olive green flowers on a white background. It is a reasonably dense flower print with not too much white, so I was pretty sure that it would not look too white in the quilt.

Since the pattern includes the sashing, it has a nice balanced look and doesn't require a complicated border. I used two of my darks as the outside border (because I couldn't decide which one I liked better).

To make photographed quilt, make six Square in the Square center blocks, twelve Broken Dishes subunits and 34 of the Mountain subunits, **Fig 2**. These subunits make up very fast (and are very portable) because they have only five and three pieces respectively! Actually this quilt goes so fast that I had originally planned to make a piece with only four Square in the Square blocks but just couldn't stop, so it grew to six.

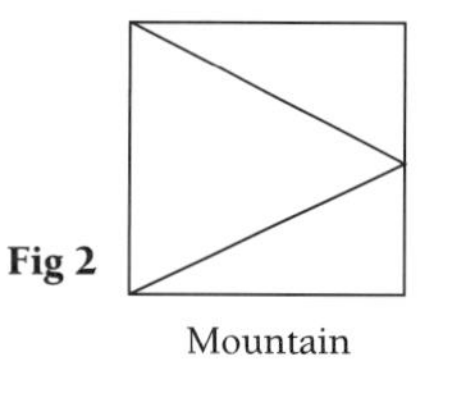

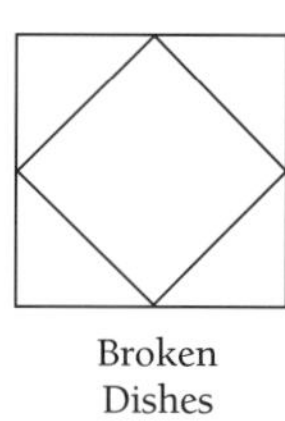

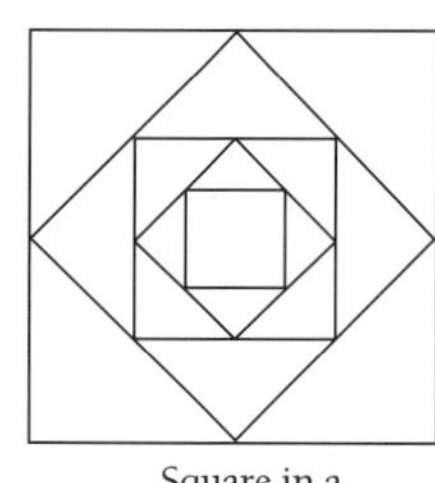

Fig 2

I.D.—*I have a confession to make. The very first quilt that I ever cut out was a Storm at Sea. The pattern I bought was for a wall hanging, but I figured, I'd just cut out a zillion more blocks and make a queen size! So I made templates, marked around them, eyeballed 1/4" seam allowance and cut out enough patches to hand piece a queen size quilt. Did you notice I said this was the first quilt I ever cut out, not the first I pieced? Or finished? Or quilted? Or slept under? Well, that's because somewhere in the deep dark recesses of the basement is a neatly labeled box with about four pieced subunits and 100,000 triangles! There are several morals to this story: 1) don't cut out all the pieces for a quilt until you try a couple of blocks to make sure you like how it looks; 2) don't commit to a technique until you are sure that you have mastered it and 3) admit when you have made a mistake, forgive yourself, learn from it and move on to the next project. Somewhere in every quilter's past is a similar story.*

R.R.R.—*There are no uncompleted projects. They are simply on hiatus.*

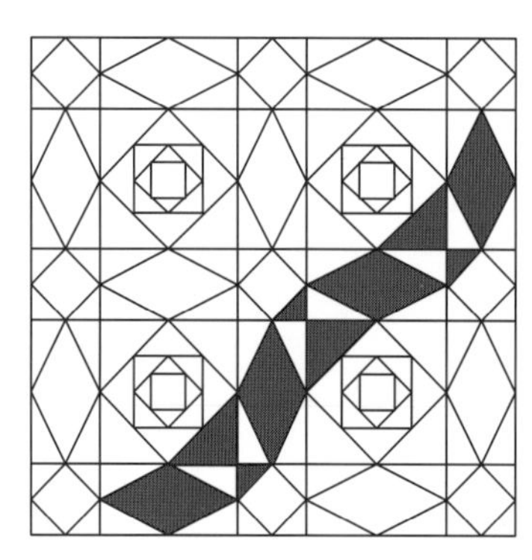

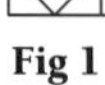

Fig 1

Prepare six Square in the Square blocks, twelve Broken Dishes subunits and 34 Mountain subunits by your chosen method.

Supplies (all fabric requirements are approximate)	
Light fabric	1/2 yd to 3/4 yd or an equivalent amount of scraps
Dark fabric	3/4 yd or an equivalent amount of scraps
Borders	1/4 yd

Notes:

1. This quilt looks wonderful either made with scraps or using only two or three fabrics. If you are trying to emphasize one or another of the secondary patterns (heart, waves, star, etc.) you might need to use some medium scraps or some bright scraps to "force" the secondary pattern to show up. Make a mock-up by pasting scraps of fabric to paper or use colored pencils, stand back and squint to help you decide.

2. If you are using only two fabrics, you may, if you wish roughly precut your fabrics as follows: (All strips are assumed to be cut crosswise from selvage to selvage and 42" to 44" wide).

Light fabric	one 2 1/2" strip, cut into 2 1/2" squares
	five 3" strips, cut into 1 3/4" by 3" rectangles
Dark fabric	four 2" strips, cut into 3 1/4" by 2" rectangles
	one 2" strip, cut into 1 1/4" by 2" rectangles
	five 2 1/2" strips, cut into 2 1/2" by 2 1/2" squares

Note: *The above will yield slightly more patches than required and some will be larger than needed.*

3. This quilt may seem a little harder to make than some of the others because we are actually making three separate sets of blocks or subunits. The individual blocks/subunits however are not too hard, so go ahead and try it! You'll be amazed at how fast it goes together.

4. Make a sample before you cut up all your fabric.

Assembly Directions

Since we are dealing with three different blocks or units, we'll consider each one separately.

Broken Dishes Subunit

1. Place a light 2 1/2" square right side up on unprinted side of base. Hold base to light and make sure that patch is centered and that you have seam allowances all around patch.

2. Fold base towards you on line between center and triangle #2 (or fold 1/4" above the line if machine stitching); trim seam allowance to a scant 1/4". Place dark fabric (if you precut your fabric use the 2" by 1 1/4" rectangles for the triangles) right side down with raw edges aligned; sew on line between patch #1 and patch #2. Smooth patch open and finger press or gently press with an iron, **Fig 3**. Add patches #3, #4, and #5 in same manner. Make twelve subunits.

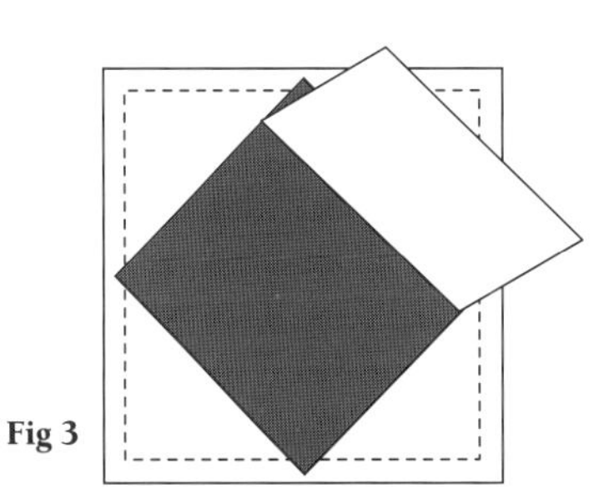
Fig 3

Mountain Subunits

1. Place a 3 1/4" by 2" dark rectangle right side up on unprinted side of base making sure that you have seam allowances all around patch #1.

2. Fold base towards you on line between patch #1 and patch #2 and pre-trim as above. Place a light 3" by 1 3/4" rectangle right side down with raw edges aligned. Stop! This long skinny triangle shape is the easiest place to make a mistake, so hold the two patches together in seam allowance and fold triangle fabric open to ensure that it will extend far enough to give a seam allowance. That is why these rectangle shapes are cut so large! It wastes a little fabric but it avoids a lot of unsewing. Sew on the line between patch #1 and patch #2. Smooth open and press or finger press. Add a triangle on other side the same way. Make 34 subunits.

3. Sew two mountain subunits together to make a diamond unit. Make seventeen diamond units.

Square in the Square

1. If you precut the dark 2 1/2" squares (see Note #2), trim six of them down to 1 1/2" squares for the block centers. Place a dark 1 1/2" square right side up over the center patch on the unprinted side of the base. Make sure that you have seam allowances all around.

2. Fold on line between patch #1 and patch #2. Pre-trim to a scant 1/4" seam allowance. If you precut your fabric, cut a light 3" by 1 3/4" rectangle into two 1 3/4" by 1 1/2" rectangles. Place one of these rectangles right side down over patch #1 aligning raw edges. Sew on line between #1 and #2. Smooth patch #2 open; press. Continue by adding three more light triangles. Add rest of patches: #6, #7, #8, and #9 are dark; #10, #11, #12, and #13 are light and #14, #15, #16, and #17 are dark. Make six blocks.

Joining Blocks and Borders

1. You should now have six Square in the Square blocks, twelve Broken Dishes subunits and seventeen Diamond units. If you have not already pressed and trimmed each unit, do so now, making sure that you leave a 1/4" seam allowance around each one. Lay out blocks in rows, following Quilt Layout. Sew units in each row together. You will find it easier when sewing the rows if seam allowances are going in opposite directions. Press all seam allowances between units away from Diamond units.

I.D.*—Let's discuss pressing seam allowances for a moment. When you are piecing on a base, the seam allowance direction is predetermined by the order in which patches are added. That means that we can't necessarily have seam allowances pressed toward the darker fabric. To minimize "shadowing" when you have seam allowances under the light patch, you may need to "grade" the fabrics. (All this means is that the light fabric seam allowance is a hair larger than the dark seam allowance.) When, however, you are sewing your blocks together you have to decide which direction to press seam allowances. On small blocks like these, sometimes seam allowances will simply refuse to go in the direction you have chosen! In that case you will have to let them go the way that they want to because they will always try to sneak back! I prefer* ***NOT*** *to press the seam allowances open because it leads to a weaker seam and frequently the stitches can be seen on the front of the quilt, but if you can't get seams to lie flat any other way, then press them open.*

2. Sew rows together. Press carefully.

3. I used two different fabrics for the borders and mitered the corners. If you don't want to miter borders, you will find other border treatments with the other quilt instructions. Mitering is one of those techniques that every quilter does a little bit differently, I think, but the end result is to join two borders in a 45 degree angle instead of having one lap over the other.

Mitered Corners

1. To miter corners, cut borders the length of the side of the quilt, plus two times the cut width of the border, plus 2". ***Example:*** If the side of the quilt measures 10" and the width of the border is 2 1/2", then cut border:

10" + 2 1/2" + 2 1/2" + 2" = 17"

2. Sew a border strip to each side of quilt using a 1/4" seam allowance; start and stop exactly 1/4" from raw edge of quilt. Backstitch a couple of stitches at beginning and end of each stitching line. See **Fig 4** for positioning of borders.

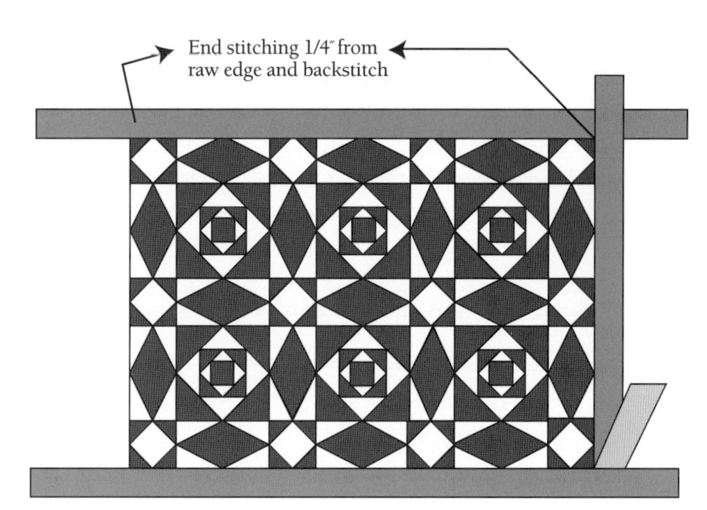

Fig 4

3. Lay quilt right side up on ironing board so that the corner that you are working on is the upper right corner. Finger press seam allowance of horizontal border towards quilt for the last inch or so before the corner (this is just temporary) and the seam allowance of the vertical border towards the border. Extend excess fabric of horizontal border to the right making sure that it is perfectly straight and smooth. Place excess fabric of the vertical border on top, making sure that the borders cross at a right angle and that everything lays nicely. (The border stitching lines should just meet—it is better to have the two stitching lines not quite meet than have them overlap.)

4. Take loose end of vertical border and fold it at a 45 degree angle under itself, lining up loose borders so that they lie perfectly even. What you should see is two border strips meeting at a 45 degree angle with excess fabric to the right. You may have to fuss with this a little to get it perfect. Carefully press the miter. Put a pin in the extra border fabric, **Fig 5**.

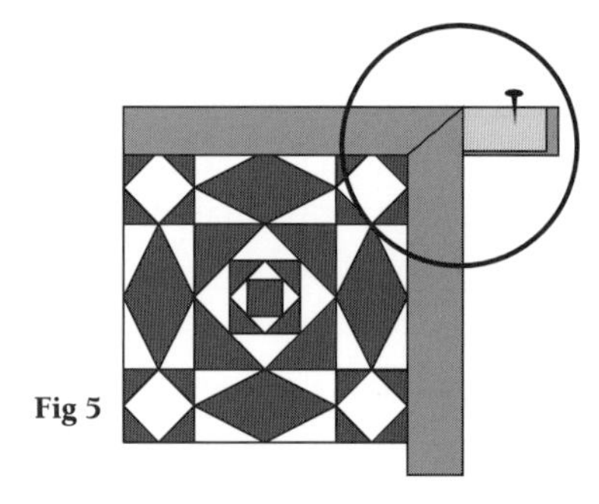

Fig 5

5. Carefully fold vertical side of quilt over horizontal side so that sewn-on borders lie exactly on top of each other; pin borders together. Pick up quilt trying not to let anything shift around, carry to sewing machine and starting at the outside edge of the borders, sew towards quilt right on the crease, **Fig 6**. Stop sewing exactly at stitching line and backstitch. Open quilt and make sure miter is flat and everything looks OK. Press. Trim miter seam to 1/4". Repeat for remaining three corners. Press seam allowances towards borders on all four sides.

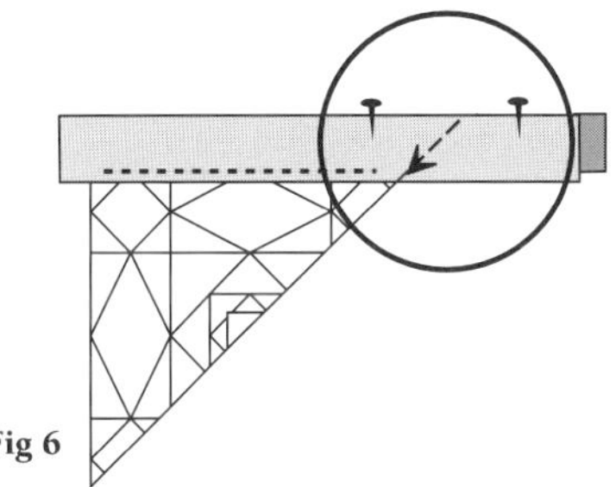

Fig 6

***I.D.**—There is an important law of miters that says "three corners will miter fine and the fourth will make you nuts." As far as I can tell, there is nothing that you can do about this other than snarl.*

Finishing the Quilt

1. Press quilt top carefully; layer with backing and batting. Quilt as desired.

2. Refer to Finishing Up, pages 59 and 60, to finish quilt.

Quilt Layout

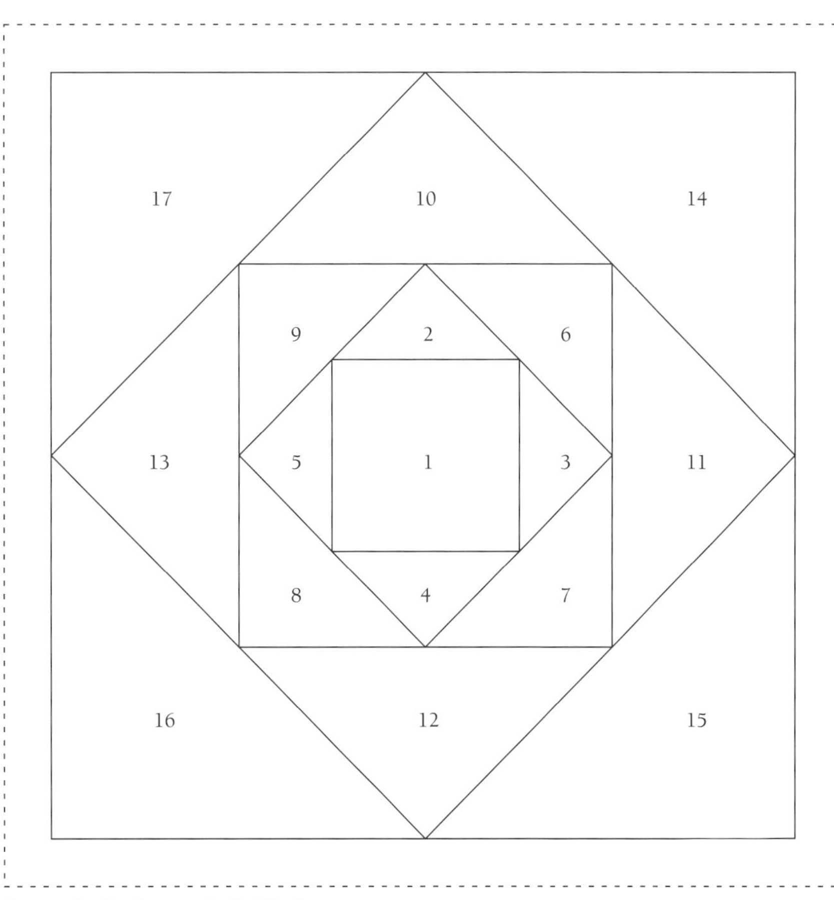

Square in the Square Quilt Block

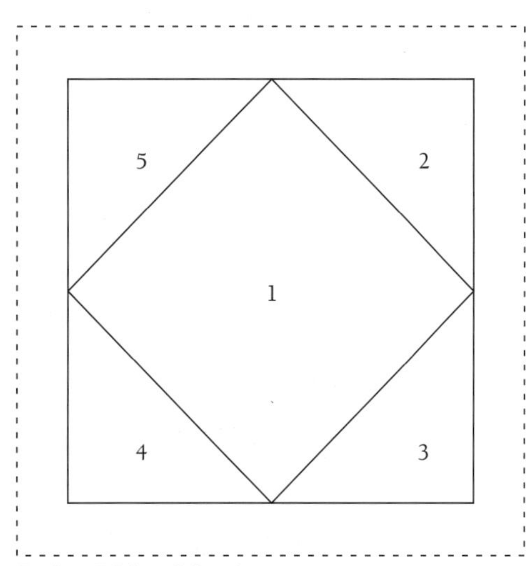

Broken Dishes Subunit

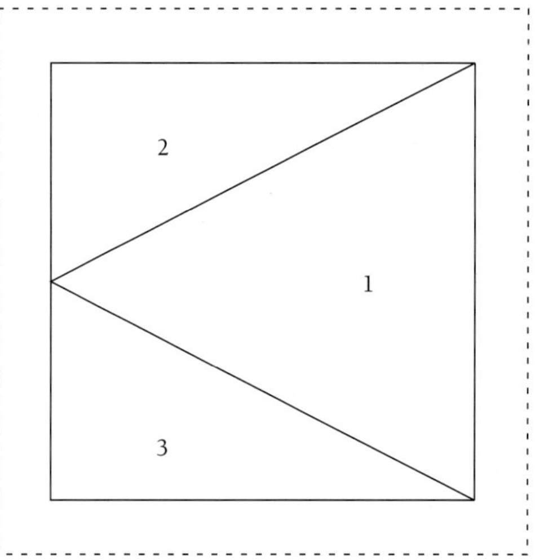

Mountain Subunit

Coloring Diagram

Crazy Patch Houses

Shown in color on page 35

Special Techniques:
Crazy Piecing

Quilt Size:
18" by 18"

Block Size:
4" square

This book wouldn't have been complete without including crazy piecing! I have been collecting homespun checks and plaids for years and this was the perfect excuse to use them. In traditional Victorian crazy-pieced quilts, the silk, satin, velvet and other fancy fabric patches were over-embroidered with intricate stitches and motifs. I decided to try some of the fancy stitches on my sewing machine instead of hand embroidery. You don't need a computerized machine to embellish—a zigzag done with interesting threads, the blind hem stitch, the stretch stitches and the other basic stitches all have possibilities! It goes without saying, that hand stitching would look terrific!

This quilt is very free-form in its creation and it is impossible for me to tell you how much yardage you need—the whole idea is to use all those odd shaped pieces of fabric that are laying around. This technique does require that you piece onto a fabric base. I started with a piece of muslin about 17" square knowing that by the time I had finished piecing and trimming, it would be smaller.

In Snail's Trail (page 26), I mentioned the "impossible seam." There are several ways to handle this when crazy piecing: 1) sew several patches together and then piece to the base; 2) cut the base into pieces before patching; 3) turn under the raw edge and stitch down and 4) leave the raw edge and then over embroider it by hand or machine. To maximize the random look of the patches and to minimize the number of "impossible" seams, pre-piecing a few patches together and then handling them as a unit works well. If you have any bits or pieces of patchwork left over from other projects that could be recut into chunks, this is a good project to use them on.

You may choose to use more than two Houses on your quilt; it's hard to say before you have pieced the background. I had originally thought I was going to use four but it made for a very crowded neighborhood when I tried it!

Prepare two or more House bases by your chosen method.

Cut a 17" or larger square of muslin.

Gather your scraps of fabric.

Assembly Directions

1. In order to make the patches go in random directions without having to deal with lots of "impossible seams," I recommend that you divide the base into four pieces. To maintain the "crazy" look, let's divide the bases unevenly, **Fig 1**.

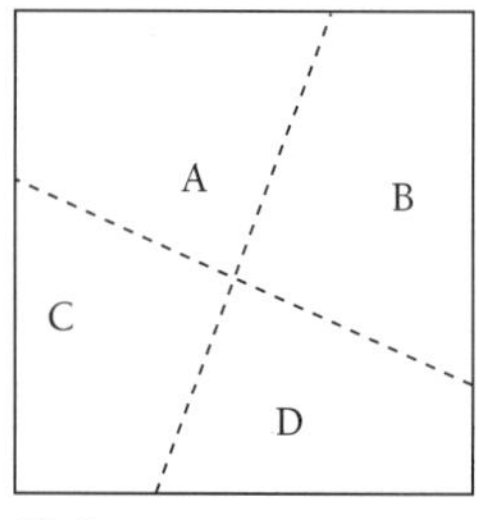

or

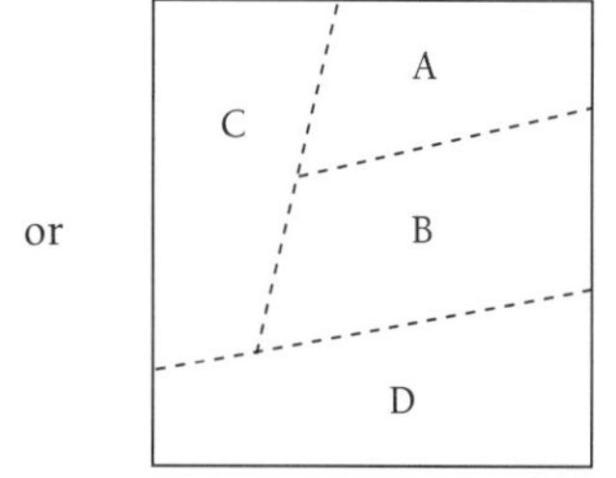

Fig 1

Label muslin pieces for easier reassembly.

2. You can start either at a corner, an edge or in the middle. If you start in the middle and piece around that patch, your results tend to have a more random look. Place the first patch right side up somewhere on the muslin. If you are using big pieces of fabric, you may want to put in a pin or use a dab of glue stick. This patch can be any shape, the patches which surround or touch it will help you to "reshape" it. Select a second patch and place it face down on one edge of the first patch, making sure that it covers one complete edge of the first patch. The seam allowances do not have to line up perfectly; you can trim excess fabric after sewing. Sew the second patch on—trim any excess seam allowance to 1/4". Smooth patch open; press or finger press. If necessary, pin to keep patch smooth and open. Continue adding patches until you have completely covered the muslin.

3. You can sew two or more patches together and then add them as a single unit. This allows you to use smaller scraps of fabric and also to "change direction."

4. If you have an "impossible seam," try one of these techniques: 1) turn under raw edge and either hand stitch it down or machine stitch it with a regular stitch right at the edge of the fold using thread that matches patch; 2) turn under raw edge, pin and then sew a decorative stitch either by hand or machine—feather stitch, narrow zigzag, etc.; 3) if you have a fabric that doesn't ravel much, you can decoratively overstitch it by hand or machine without turning under a seam allowance.

***I.D.**—This will either be the most difficult or the easiest quilt that you will ever make—depending on your mental attitude! If you approach this as FUN and give yourself permission to "cut loose" with fabrics, shapes, stitches, threads and techniques, you will have a great time! There are no points to match! There is no predetermined size! If things don't meet, then you are doing it right! By the way, it is almost impossible to over-embellish a crazy quilt so try every stitch on your machine and every hand embroidery stitch you have ever wondered about! The great thing is that you rarely wind up doing more than 3 or 4 inches of a stitch at a time, so if you don't like the stitch you are not committed to miles of it! This is a fun project for kids—iron a paper-backed fusible such as Wonder-Under™ or HeatnBond® to back off fabric scraps. Let them cut out shapes, fuse them down and decorate with paint and glue using ribbon, beads, sequins and "found" objects.*

5. Crazy-patch other pieces of muslin, trying to keep patches looking random in shape, size and direction. Trim patches even with edges of muslin. Sew the four muslin sections back together. You will find that the muslin pieces have "warped" and changed shape and probably don't want to fit together perfectly anymore—no problem. Just sew them together and trim the seam allowance if necessary to 1/4". This is probably pretty "unsquare" at this point, so either using a quilter's square ruler, a piece of cardboard or something with a nice right angle corner, square the base up. My 17" piece of muslin finally reduced itself to about 13 1/2" before I was happy with it.

6. Machine-embroider some decorative stitching along a few of the edges of the patches at this point. You may add more stitching after the houses have been added.

7. The House pattern is very easy to piece. First piece the door and windows, then the "grass" and finally the roof. As you can see from the photograph (page 45), I used the House pattern both right side up and mirror imaged. For a mirror image, trace block carefully onto tracing paper so that block can be seen from both side of the paper.

8. Lay #1 piece of house fabric right side up on the unprinted side of base making sure that it has seam allowances all around. Fold base back on line between patches #1 and #2 (or 1/4" above line if you are machine piecing); pre-trim raw edge to a scant 1/4". Lay "door" fabric right side down over #1 aligning raw edges. Sew on printed line and smooth patch open. Continue adding pieces of house fabric and windows through patch #7. Patches #1, #3, #5, and #7 are House fabric; patches #2, #4, and #6 are door and window fabric.

9. Patch #8 is the grass or a porch in front of the house. If you want your House to sit right on your background do not add this patch, simply trim the block off 1/4" below the door and windows. Patch #9 is more house fabric. In one house, I decided to let the roof line extend down to the top of the door and windows, combining patches #9 and #10. The dotted line on the base can be used as part of the roof line to make the house seem more dimensional. After all the patches are added, you can hand or machine sew (stem stitch or narrow zigzag) this line if desired. The two corner triangles are "sky" or background.

10. Trim House blocks leaving 1/4" seam allowance all around. The uppermost House in the quilt has the seam allowances folded under and is buttonhole stitched to background. The other House was simply zigzagged over the raw edges—I left the 1/4" seam allowance on the second block because I wanted this to be a bigger house. There is a lot of room for "custom decorating" here.

11. I tried a couple of different borders on this quilt before I was happy with how it looked. When you are crazy piecing, it is impossible to decide in advance what border treatment will look best!

12. After layering backing, batting and quilt top, add more decorative stitching and embellishment to hold everything together—in this case the decorative stitching is also the quilting. If you have been collecting buttons, little charms and other embellishments, this is the perfect quilt to use them on. If you used fancy fabrics, a little beading and some sequins would also be fun.

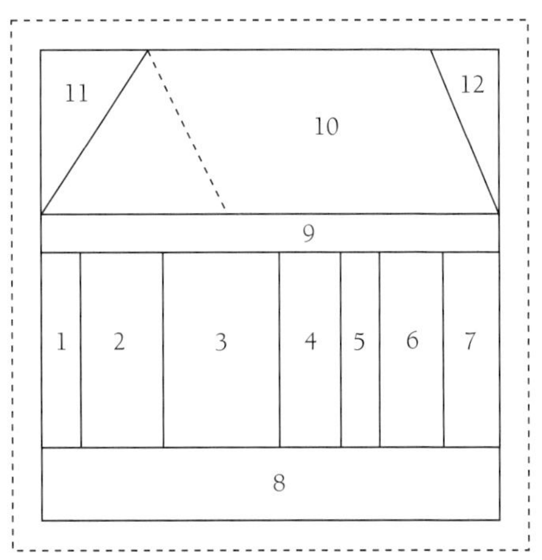

Quilt Block

continued

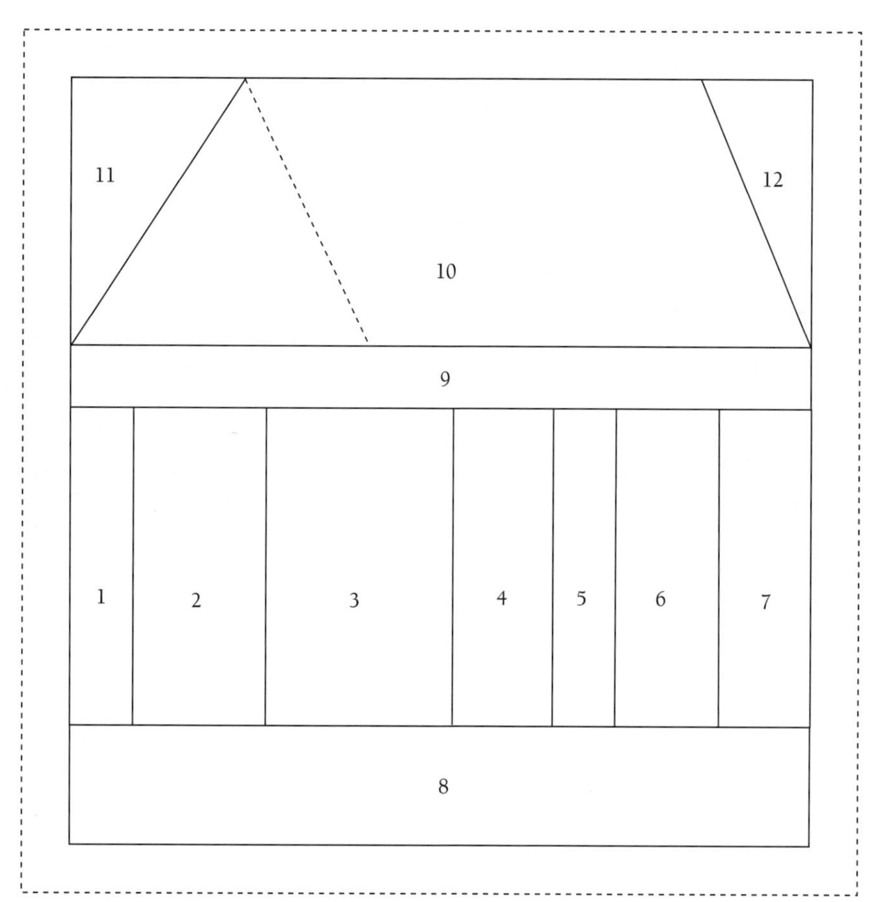

Quilt Block

Bonus Blocks, Orphan Blocks and the Two Dreaded "D" Words...

Made by Pat Coulter

Shown in color on page 34

Special Techniques:
New Blocks from Old Friends

Quilt Size:
9 1/2" square

Block Size:
2" square

A serendipitous result of making quilts are the bonuses! Not the bonus of suddenly making lots of new friends - both quilters and people who want you to make them a quilt; not the bonus of having wonderful quilts on your walls and beds; and not the bonus of having a great reason for buying all those wonderful fabrics. But rather the bonus of suddenly having extra blocks that didn't quite make it into your quilt and also the bonus of finding new patterns and designs. I can hear you saying, "she's crazy, why are leftover blocks a bonus?" Well, it's all in how you look at it. Everyone who makes quilts sooner or later makes a block or two that turns out the wrong size or just lies there and looks boring or took so long to make that you know you are never going to make another or ..., or ... You can take those "orphans" and hide them away or you can do what I do, hang them on the bulletin board and let them live with you for awhile (sometimes a long while!).

Some of the most wonderful quilts I have seen are scrap samplers where both the fabrics and the blocks were "left-overs." In making the samples for this book, I generated several orphans—I accidentally made a star for the Sampler center a 12" square instead of 6", a Wheel block that never made it into the quilt, and four Pineapple blocks in colors that turned out to be exceedingly boring. These are hanging up along with some extras from previous projects—one day they will become a scrap sampler.

There are other fun things to do with orphans. My Computer Online Guild runs a monthly orphan drawing. Everyone who has an orphan that they are tired of looking at puts their name in the hat and one lucky person wins them all. Your orphan is probably someone else's masterpiece. Sometimes I put an orphan on the back of a quilt and if it has enough white or muslin in it, I use it as a signature block, if not, it's simply decoration. From time to time, you may need a block for a group quilt and you will have a block all ready. I have also used orphans as pockets on dresses and aprons, Christmas tree ornaments, pillows, medallion centers etc. And last but not least, you may find that a block that you made several years ago will suddenly inspire you to make a wonderful quilt that you might never have thought of otherwise!

R.R.R.—*Not all quilts are masterpieces, some just cover holes in the wall.*

OK, now that we are excited by our mistakes, what other bonuses are there? Well, I think one of the fun things to do is to take a quilt pattern and play with it—recolor it, chop it in half, chop it in quarters, add lines, delete lines, stretch it, warp it. Remarkable things can happen! We have already done some of this in the Pinwheels in the Garden quilt (page 22) and in the center of the Sampler Medallion (page 54), so let's play a little more.

Did you happen to notice that the middle of the Storm at Sea (the Square in the Square block, page 43 and the Snail's Trail block, page 30) are the same except for the four-patch in the center of the Snail, **Fig 1**?

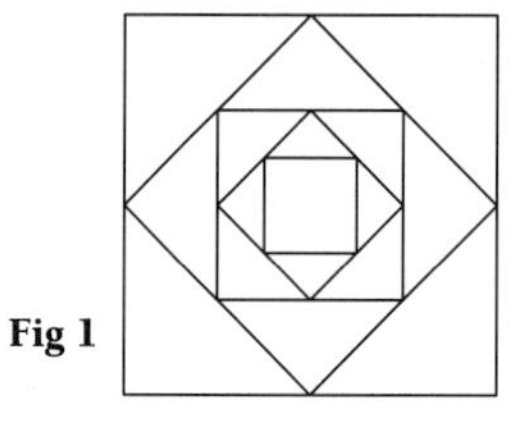
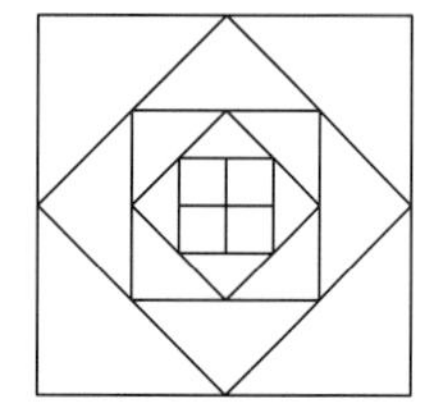

Fig 1

So we could say that the Square in the Square block is really the Snail's Trail recolored. (Well, actually I didn't notice it right off the bat either.) Let's play with the Snail's Trail first and do some recolorations and see what happens.

The Snail's Trail, when set with all the Snail's of one color meeting in the middle is called the Virginia Reel, **Fig 2**. Or if you color the last four triangles differently than the Snail, the block looks as if it's set on point, **Fig 3**.

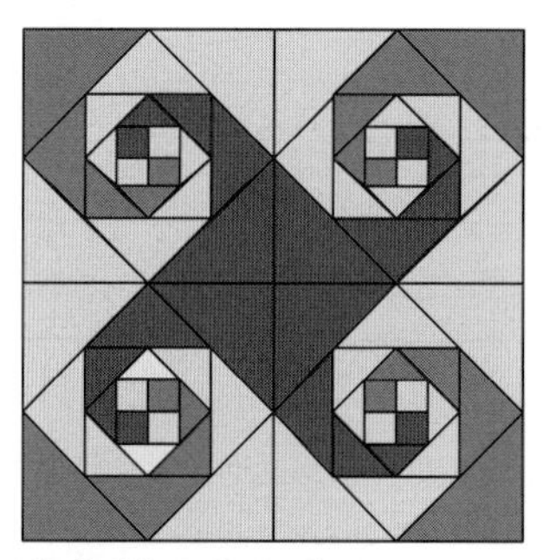

Fig 2- Virginia Reel

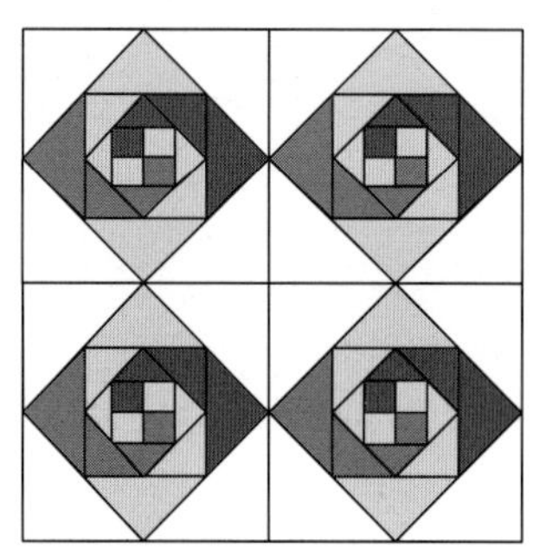

Fig 3

Now, let's recolor the Snail so that it doesn't spin anymore and so that it looks a little more like the Square in the Square. Interestingly, we begin to get lots of diagonal movement.

When four of these are put together, **Fig 4**, it sort of looks like an X. Can we also get O's? How about X's and O's in a nine patch (three by three) set, **Fig 5**? Do you see a tic-tac-toe board with both X winning and O winning? Squint and look only at the darks, see the X's in the upper left, upper right, center, etc. Now concentrate only on the lights. Do you see light O's in the upper left, upper right, center, etc.? I also see the possibilities of stars.

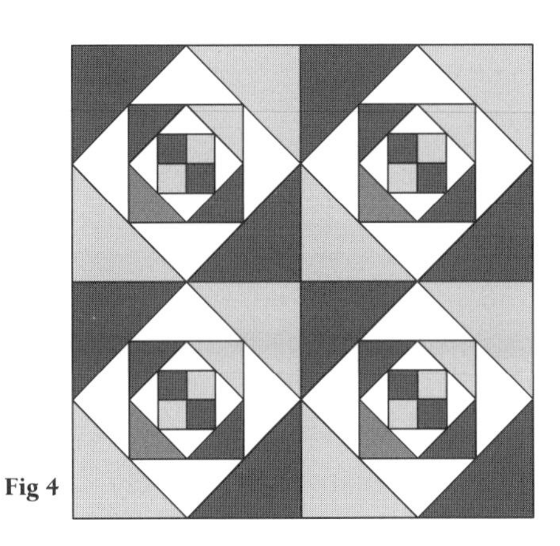
Fig 4

Fig 5

What happens if we chop the block in half, **Fig 6**? Hmmm, might make an OK border, but it's not too exciting right now—let's tuck this away in an idea file for a later time when it'll be perfect.

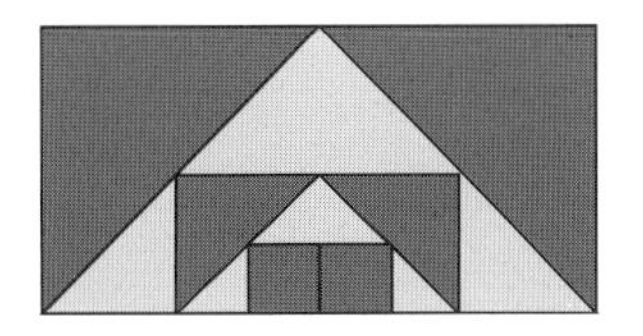
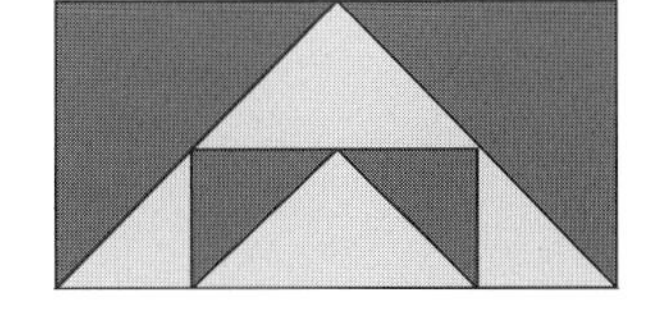
Fig 6

Well OK, how about if we cut the block in quarters, **Fig 7**? That's not bad but that little square in the corner sort of annoys me, so let's get rid of it, **Fig 8**. It looks like a Mama and a baby goose. Wait! What if we put that little square back and chop it diagonally—three generations of geese, **Fig 9**! Can we make that four, **Fig 10**?

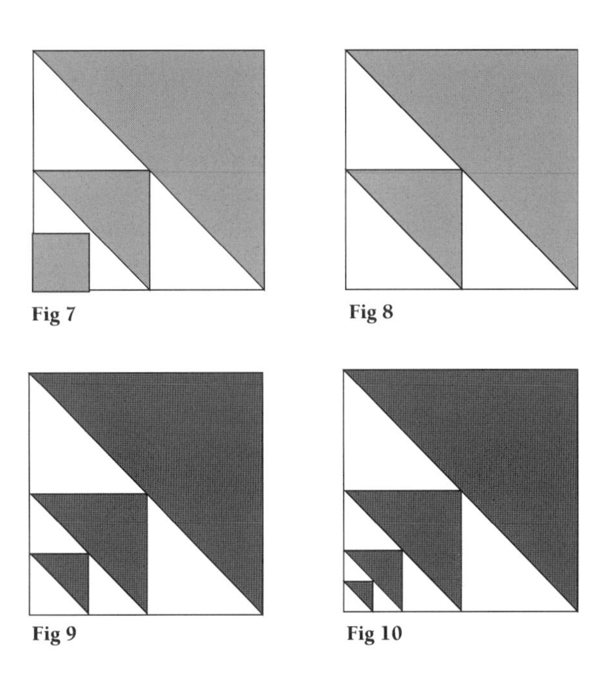

Want to draw this yourself? OK, draw a square any size. Draw one diagonal. Draw the two sides of the square that fit exactly between the diagonal and the corner of the original square. Draw the diagonal in the new square (in the same direction as the original diagonal). Now draw a third square that exactly fits between the second diagonal and the corner of the original square. Wow! You could make a whole quilt that's just one block.

Oh, by the way, the two "D" words are DRAFTING and DESIGN and you have just learned some basics of both. See, that didn't hurt at all.

My friend, Pat Coulter, made her little quilt by setting her geese alternately with plain setting squares. She cut plain blocks the same size as her unfinished pieced blocks (2 1/2"). So, if you need to turn out a quilt quickly or want to use a particular block but don't want to make a lot of them, try using an alternate plain block.

Prepare five bases by your chosen method.

Supplies (all fabric requirements are approximate)	
Background fabric	1/4 yd or fat quarter or equivalent light colored scraps (includes borders)
Geese fabric	1/8 yd or equivalent scraps

Notes:

1. You will need five scraps about 3 1/2" by 2" for the biggest geese in the blocks. The other patches are so small that just about any little smidgen of fabric will do!

2. Border strips will be 2 1/2" by 11" (shorter, if you don't miter the corners) and plain squares will be 2 1/2" square (including seam allowance). I prefer to cut these after I have made my pieced blocks and measured them. Make sure to set aside enough background fabric if you are not cutting these until after your piecing is completed.

3. Make a sample block.

Assembly Directions

1. Place a small scrap of fabric right side up on unprinted side of base over patch #1. Hold base to light to make sure that you have seam allowances all around patch.

2. Fold base towards you on line between #1 and #2 (or a scant 1/4" above line if you are sewing by machine); pre-trim raw edge to a scant 1/4". Place geese fabric for patch #2 right side down aligning raw edges; sew on the line between #1 and #2. Smooth patch open; press or finger press.

3. Add background patches (#3 and #4) on either side of first goose. Continue adding patches following numbers on base. Patches #5 and #8 are the other two geese.

4. If you want only two geese in each block, treat patches #1, #2, #3, and #4 as a single patch, placing a piece of background fabric large enough to cover all these patches right side up on unprinted line of base, fold on line between #4 and #5; pre-trim.

5. Make five geese blocks and trim making sure that you have 1/4" seam allowance all around. They should measure 2 1/2" with seam allowance. Cut four 2 1/2" background squares and lay out the blocks, alternating pieced blocks and plain blocks. Sew blocks into rows; sew rows together to make quilt top.

6. Cut borders 2" wide. Sew borders to quilt following directions for mitering corners in Storm at Sea, page 42, to miter corners. You might also choose to use any of the other border choices described in this book.

7. This quilt is quilted very simply—in the ditch between the blocks and around each goose. The plain blocks and the borders were left unquilted but these would be fun to hand or machine quilt!

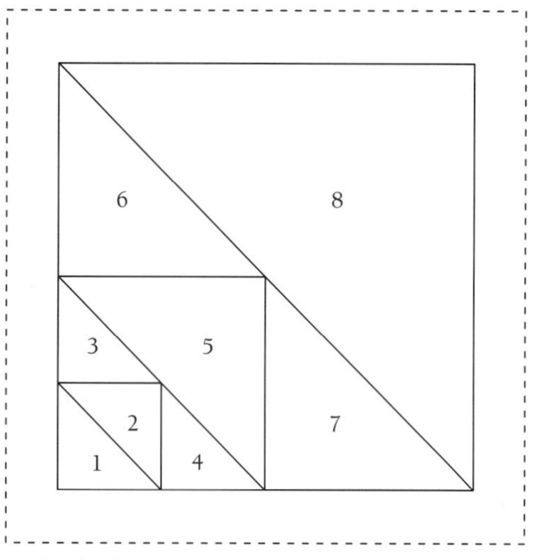

Quilt Block

Quilt Layout

Coloring Diagram

"Tornado" - Medallion Sampler Quilt

Shown in color on front cover

Special Techniques:
Playing with the Set

Quilt Size:
26" by 22"

Block Sizes:
2" square and 4" square

To me, a sampler quilt is a bigger challenge than any other quilt pattern, block or set. Notice I said challenge, not problem! There are wonderful opportunities to play with color, fabric, set and block selection; to experiment without committing to a whole quilt of one block or color choice; to try things that you have been curious about; and to truly make a quilt that is unique! You have to be prepared to have a few "oopsies" along the way—blocks that don't quite work, fabrics that looked terrific on the bolt but not in the quilt, layouts that leave you cold. I designed this sampler to give you a lot of flexibility in block design and set. All the blocks finish at 4" or 2" (except the medallion center Star) so that you can add or delete bits and pieces. The medallion center is a 6" block which is bordered, set on point, and "squares up" to 10". I encourage you to make this quilt uniquely yours by varying the blocks and setting!

I.D.*—Let's talk about "design walls" and auditioning fabrics and blocks. I firmly believe that it is very important during the construction of a quilt to view the blocks. If you have the luxury of a sewing room or studio of your very own, then making a design wall is a cinch. Take some flannel or sturdy batting (I use some stuff that I think is supposed to go in outdoor clothing and I no longer know why I bought it) and either thumbtack it to the wall or back it with some old fabric and hang it from the molding. The flannel's natural fuzziness or nap will "grab" patches and blocks. You can pat your pieces onto the "wall" and stand back and look at them. I also have several "portable" walls which are nothing more than foam core board that I bought at the artist's supply store. You can pin into the foam core with straight pins. A friend pointed out that you can cover the foam core with flannel and have the best of all possible worlds: fuzziness to hold small pieces, pinning for larger pieces, as well as portability! Now that you have a design wall, you can audition fabrics, blocks and sets.*

The first step is to decide on a general color scheme or mood for the quilt. This can range from very controlled—say, all shades of blue from light to dark—to two or three colors to a total scrap look. You could decide to "set a mood" rather than picking specific colors. Perhaps an old-fashioned look with all sorts of plaids, or a very modern feeling with lots of brights or an Amish feeling using a black background and solids. I decided on two fabrics - one an "upholstery" type stripe and one with medium flowers. That focused the quilt on peaches and greens as a general color scheme. I pulled out all the fabrics that I owned that could even remotely be called peach and green. In order to make a quilt have "life", you need to have fabrics which range from very dark through very light, so I tossed in a couple with black backgrounds and a navy blue. The colors presented a challenge to me because I rarely use green.

R.R.R.*—Go buy the ugliest fabric you can find in the ugliest color available and make it the basis of your next quilt.*

I didn't use all the fabrics that I had pulled out and I did have to find some additional fabrics as the piece developed—but you have to start somewhere.

I recommend that you make the bases for the medallion center and construct the center first. Then make a few geese and three or four of the individual blocks. As you make these blocks, pin them to your design wall and see if they are "working." Don't be afraid to make changes as you go. I discovered that the fabric that I had chosen for the big triangles around the center star looked less than wonderful after I laid out some geese and a few blocks, so I replaced it. Make sure that you move back at least five feet and look at your quilt. You'll be amazed at the difference.

R.R.R.*—You'll never be closer to the quilt than you are right now, unless you are asleep on it!*

To make the sampler as pictured you will need the following muslin or paper bases:

Type of block/unit	# and cut size of bases	Where used
Mountain subunit (2" finished) page 44	four 2 1/2" squares	Medallion Star points
(1" finished) page 57	eight 1 1/2" squares	small Pinwheel in corners
Wheel subunit (2" finished) page 25	four 2 1/2" squares	Medallion Star corners
	four 2 1/2" squares	Pinwheel block
Geese (2" finished) page 58	fourteen 2 1/2" squares	two sides of medallion
	five 2 1/2" squares	outer border
Broken Dishes subunit (2" finished) page 44	four 2 1/2" squares	Broken Dishes block
	one 2 1/2" square	Medallion Star center
Pineapple (4" finished) page 38	one 4 1/2" square	Pineapple block
Snail's Trail (4" finished) page 30	one 4 1/2" block	Snail block
Chevron (4" finished) page 57	one 4 1/2" square	Chevron block
House (4" finished) page 48	one 4 1/2" square	House block
Log Cabin (4" finished) page 16	one 4 1/2" square	Log Cabin block
Square in the Square (4" finished) page 43	one 4 1/2" square	Square in a Square block

Supplies (all fabric requirements are approximate)	
Background	1/4 yd to 1/2 yd
Border	1/4 yd
Blocks	3/4 yd to 1 yd total or equivalent scraps

Notes:

1. If you are making a multi-fabric scrappy sampler, just gather up your scraps, making sure that you have lights and darks as well as mediums. You will need some larger pieces for the setting triangles and plain blocks, as well as the borders. If you are making a sampler with a limited number of fabrics, then I would estimate that 1 3/4 to 2 yds of fabric total will be adequate.

2. Do not precut your borders, setting triangles for the medallion center, plain rectangles and squares, but remember when you are rough cutting shapes for the blocks that you will need these pieces later for finishing the quilt.

3. Keep an open mind about which fabrics and blocks go where.

4. In the directions below, I will be referring to the quilts where these subunits and blocks are described in detail. Please review those sections and the General Directions, pages 6 and 7.

Assembly Directions

Medallion Star Center

1. Make bases for four 2" Mountain subunits, one 2" Broken Dishes subunit, and four 2" Wheel subunits. The Broken Dishes subunit and the Mountain subunits are pieced as usual: Patch #1 fabric placed right side up on unprinted side of base, pre-trim, place next patch right side down with raw edges aligned, sew, smooth open, and press. (See Storm at Sea, page 41, for specifics.)

2. The four corners of the Medallion Star are Wheel subunits with patches #1 and #2 treated as a single patch. Simply place a patch right side up on unprinted side of base treating #1 and #2 as a single patch. Pre-trim on the line between #1#2 and #3 and proceed as usual.

3. Lay out the nine subunits for the Star, **Fig 1**; sew together. Measure the Star—it should measure 6" plus a seam allowance (6 1/2" using a 1/4" seam allowance).

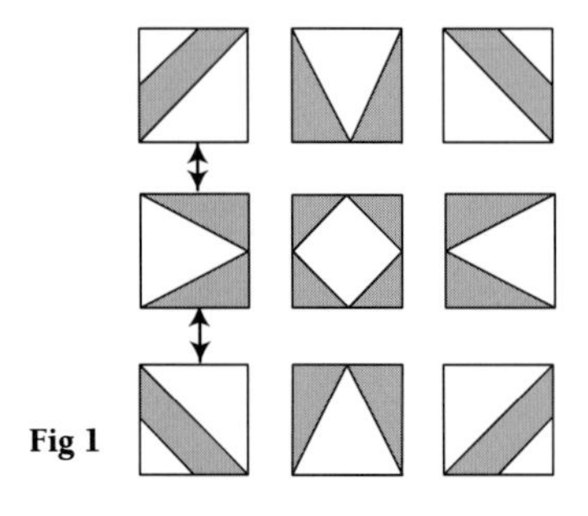
Fig 1

4. Cut strips 1" wide from dark scraps for the narrow border. If you decide to miter this border (see Storm at Sea, page 42, for mitering directions), cut strips 9 1/2" to 10" long. Otherwise, you need two strips 6 1/2" long and two strips 8 1/2" long. Sew the narrow border to all four sides. Measure the Medallion Star again—it should now be 7" plus a seam allowance (7 1/2"). The Star and the narrow border together need to be 7" plus a seam allowance (7 1/2") for the center to come out the right size. If your Star is a smidgen larger or smaller, you can adjust the narrow border to compensate.

5. If you know what fabric you are using for the setting triangles, you can cut them now and attach them to the Star, **Fig 2**. Otherwise leave this step and step 6 until after you have made some Geese and a few blocks. Cut two 5 1/2" squares of fabric and subcut along one diagonal. The long edge of each triangle, which is bias, will be sewn to the side of the Star block. This bias edge will be a trifle large. Find center of side of star block and match it to center of bias edge; sew carefully with a 1/4" seam allowance. (See Pinwheels in the Garden, page 24, for detailed instructions.) If you are sewing by machine, sew with Star block on top to minimize stretching the bias. Press carefully and measure. The star medallion center should measure 10" plus seam allowance (10 1/2"). If necessary, you may carefully square this up making sure that you leave a 1/4" seam allowance all around.

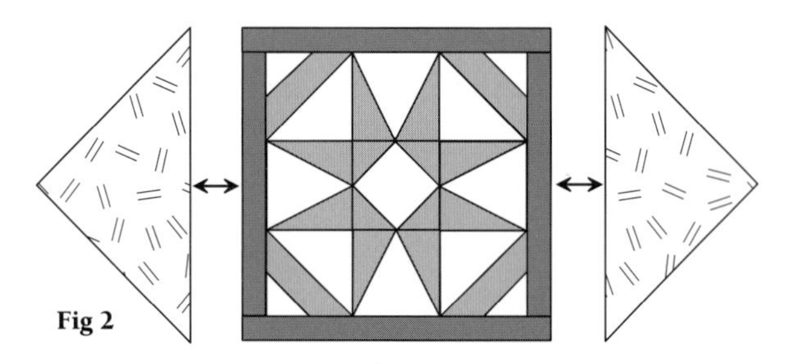
Fig 2

6. Stop! If your center does not measure the right size, let's figure out what to do about it! If it is a smidgen too large—can you make the narrow border around the star even narrower? Did you cut your setting triangles too large and float the center? Can you trim down the float? If it is too small, can you add a narrow border around the center? Do not be discouraged or give up! If you make adjustments, write them down on the Quilt Layout on page 58.

Making the Geese

1. Each Geese unit is composed of two geese. I made light- and medium-colored Geese with dark "backgrounds". They also look wonderful done with dark geese and light backgrounds. Cut a 1 3/4" by 2 3/4" rectangle and place it right side up on unprinted side of base over patch #1. Hold in place with a dab of glue stick. Fold base back on line between #1 and #2 (or 1/4" above the line if you are machine sewing) and trim to a scant 1/4". Place a 2 1/4" by 1 1/4" rectangle right

side down, raw edges aligned; sew. Smooth open and press. Add patch #3 the same way. Patch #4 is next goose followed by #5 and #6.

2. Make three or four blocks and lay out the Star center, the Geese and any other finished blocks on your design wall. Is it working? Is there too much of one color? Not enough variety? Does it need a little sparking up? If it looks like it's dying up there on the wall, try adding "zinger"—I added some yellow. To make the "zinger" look like it "belongs" in the quilt, use a little bit of it in several places, three or four usually does it.

Photographed quilt has a total of nineteen Geese blocks (five are used in the border).

3. Make the rest of the blocks: one House, one Pineapple, one Snail's Trail, one Chevron, one Log Cabin, one Square in the Square and four Broken Dishes. Pin everything to your design wall. The plain rectangles on the top and bottom are cut 2 1/2" by 4 1/2" (finished, 2" by 4). Originally I had planned for these to be more Geese, but as my quilt developed, the Geese just didn't work. But, they might look wonderful in your quilt—try it. The plain rectangles to the left and right of the Geese are also cut 2 1/2" by 4 1/2". Two corner rectangles are cut 6 1/2" by 4 1/2" (finished 6" by 4") and two corner squares are cut 4 1/2"x 4 1/2" (finished 4"). Think of the Quilt Layout as a series of spaces that need to be filled with something—blocks, background, half blocks, whatever and let yourself play with the arrangement.

Borders

The borders are finished at 2" wide. For visual interest, I decided to use some Geese in the borders and to make two little pinwheel type blocks, using 1" Mountain subunits on next page, **Fig 3**. You can, of course, make plain borders and attach them using any of the border techniques mentioned in previous sections. Measure quilt, decide on borders and use border techniques to add your borders.

Finishing

I went to town quilting my sampler and used all kinds of metallic and rayon threads. Some blocks have quilting in the ditch, some are outlined 1/8" to 1/4" from the seam—whatever seemed right! I hope you had fun planning and making this sampler and that your mind is brimming over with ideas for more quilts!

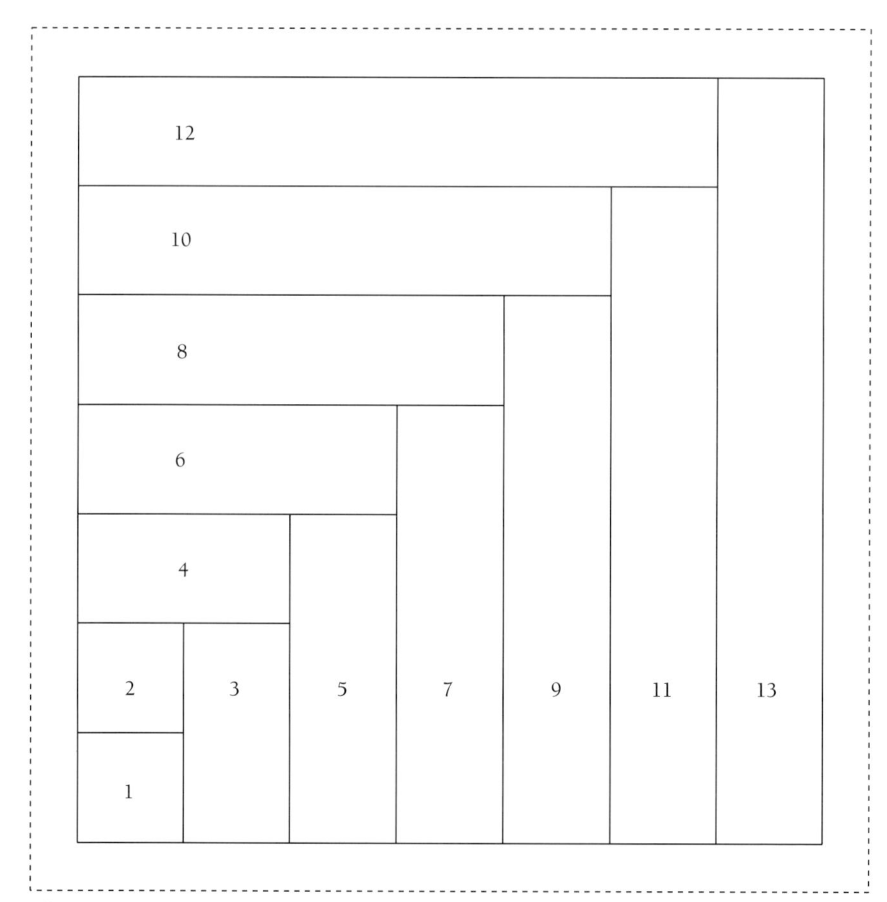

Chevron Quilt Block

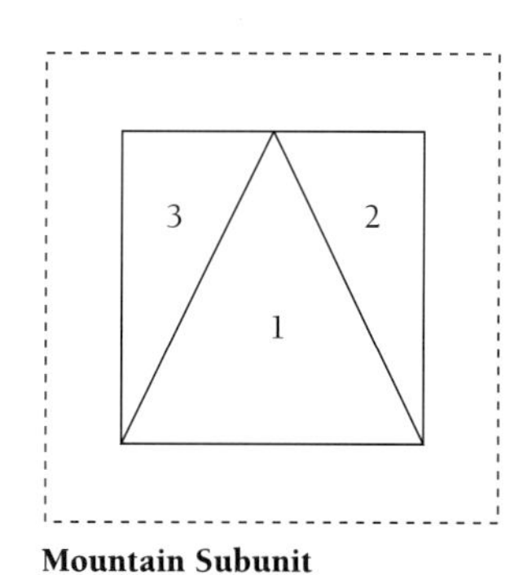

Mountain Subunit

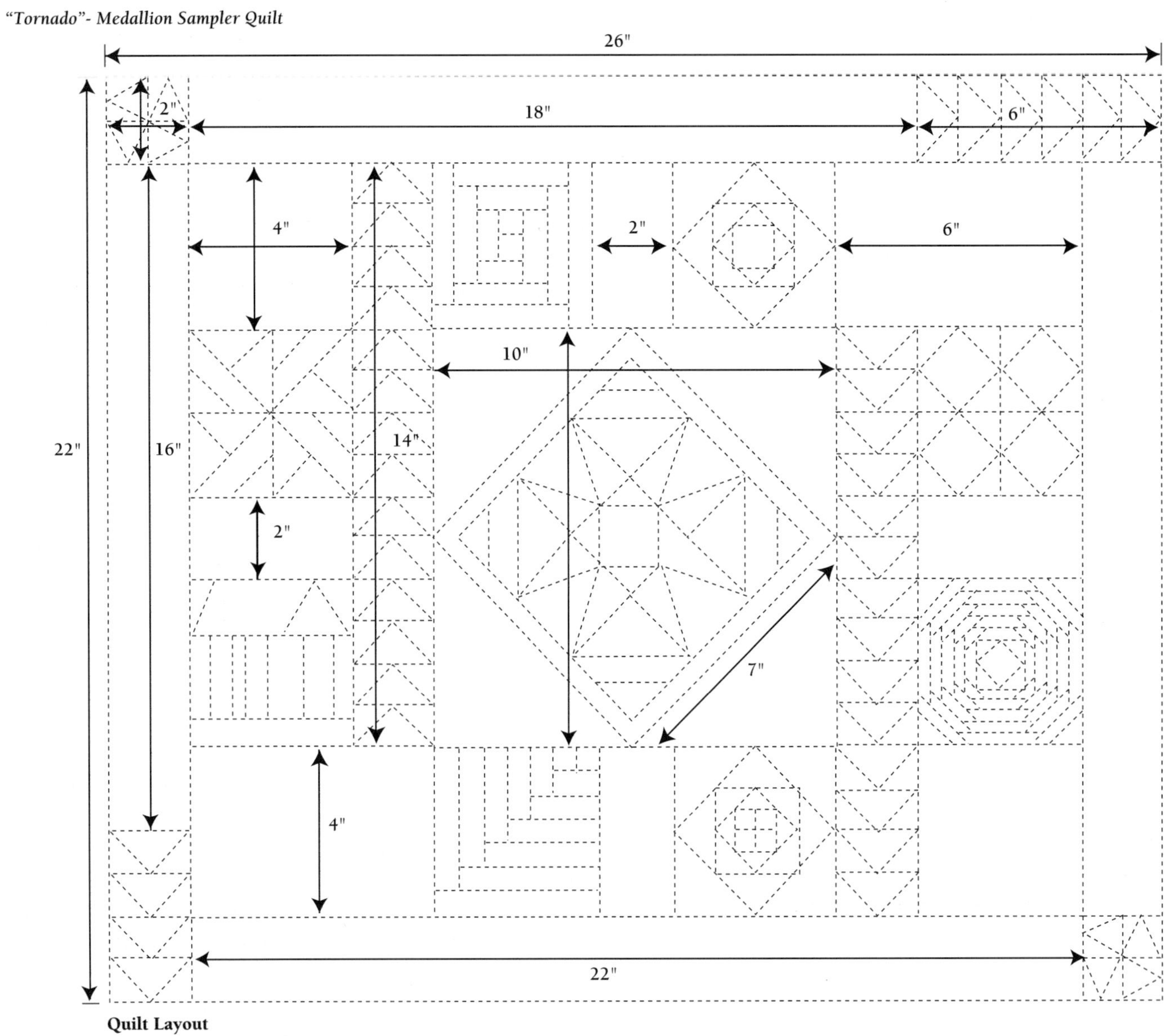

Quilt Layout

Fig 3

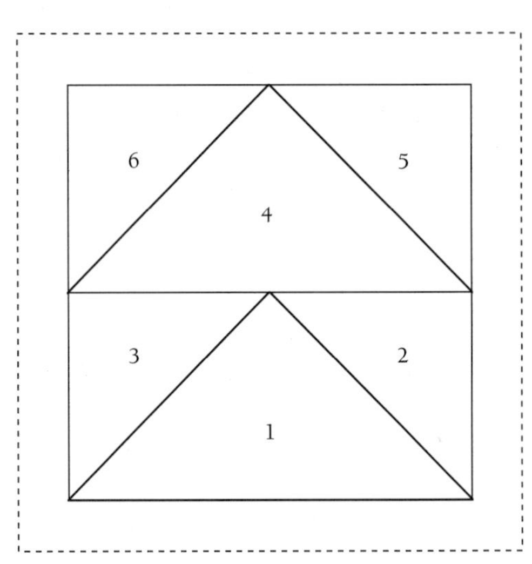

Flying Geese Block

Finishing Up

A few final words need to be said about binding and quilting. There are various ways to bind the outside edges of your little quilt. In the Tree Ornaments chapter we left the batting and raw edges unfinished. This is certainly the easiest way to finish something since it's unfinished, but perhaps it's not really appropriate for a quilt. We did two envelope finishes—one in Birds of a Feather Chevron, page 20, where we layered the quilt with the batting, backing and top and sewed all around and turned right side out. A similar finish was used on the Pineapple quilt, page 37. The difference being that we sewed a narrow border of a contrasting fabric around the top, used the same fabric for the back, sewed them together using the envelope technique and then stitched in the ditch next to the seam joining the narrow border to the quilt top. This made it look like we had applied a separate binding to the quilt.

If you wish to quilt your quilt and apply a separate binding, cut a backing and batting about 2" bigger all around than the quilt. Lay the backing right side down on the table, lay the batting on top of it and then the quilt top right side up. Either thread baste or safety pin baste to keep layers together. Because these mini quilts are so small, they require very little quilting. You may find it easier to machine quilt if you have used muslin bases because the extra layer of fabric makes hand quilting a little harder, or you might choose to machine quilt the center of the quilt and hand quilt the borders. Most of the quilts in this book are "stitched in the ditch" (right next to the seam on the side without the seam allowances) and have some decorative quilting in the borders.

I.D.—*No, I am not avoiding the question of what batting to use! I think that the batting you choose depends on whether you are hand quilting or machine quilting; how closely together you will quilt and what looks and feels good to YOU! There are many excellent battings available and I recommend that you experiment with different types. Quilting a mini quilt is a good time to experiment. If you discover that you don't like a batting, you haven't committed yourself to a zillion hours of quilting. In general, bonded polyester battings are easier to needle, don't need to be quilted more closely than every 4" to 6" and give a puffier look. Cotton and cotton/poly (generally 80% cotton, 20% polyester) are harder to needle, need to be quilted more closely, may need to be pre-soaked (varies by brand) and give a flatter, more traditional look to your quilts. Batting choice is a very personal thing. (By the way there are also wool and silk battings available.)*

Now you can add ruffles to the edge, prairie points or make your little mini quilt into a pillow top. If you want to finish the top more traditionally there are several methods for applying bindings. Here are the directions for applying a double fold, straight grain binding. (If you have a favorite method of applying binding, then go ahead and use it.)

Binding

1. The width of the binding on a quilt is a function of the size of the quilt and what visually seems to look best. As a general rule, the smaller the quilt the narrower the binding. On a Queen/King size quilt you frequently see bindings that are 1/2" or wider; on small quilts like these 1/4" to 3/8" is appealing. Cut your binding strips according to the following rule:

(finished width x 4) + 1/2"

2. For a 1/4"-wide binding, cut strips about 1 1/2" wide. I usually cut my binding strips a bit larger (1/8" to 1/4") than the formula, because I tend to sew a generous 1/4" seam and to allow for the fabric that is taken up folding the binding over the edge of the quilt and batting. I'm not trying to waffle on the width, but the fabric used in the quilt and the batting can make a difference, so you may want to experiment a little as you make bindings.

3. You may cut your strips on the crosswise grain or the lengthwise grain of the fabric. The strip length should equal the length of the side plus about 2". If you have to piece together strips to get sufficient length, it is best to do that with a diagonal seam—it's stronger and less visible. Just follow **Fig 1** to piece strips together:

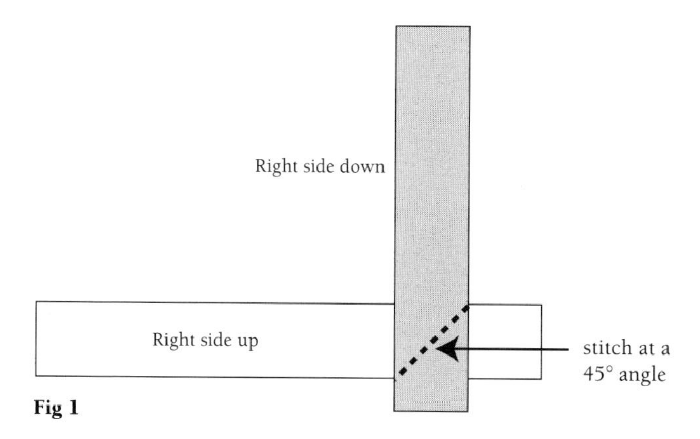

Fig 1

4. Fold strips in half lengthwise wrong sides together and press.

5. Lay the quilt sandwich on a flat surface right side up and pin perpendicular to the edge. Lay binding over the edge with the raw edges aligned, **Fig 2**; sew (1/4" seam allowance) from one edge of quilt to the other, removing pins as you get to them. Trim edge of quilt top, batting and backing equal to calculated finished width of binding plus a scant 1/8". (It's real important that the batting extends all the way to the edge of the binding to improve the look of the quilt as well as make the binding more durable.)

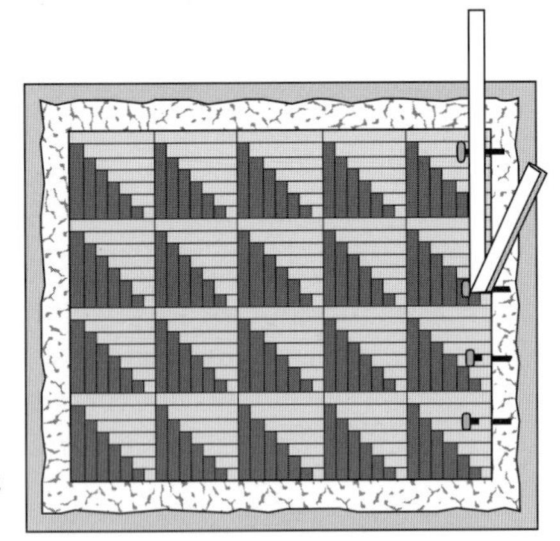
Fig 2

6. Smooth binding open and turn folded edge over to back of quilt so that it just covers stitching line. (If backing/batting is just too fat, trim it very slightly). Sew with a small whip stitch to the back of the quilt using thread that matches the binding. Make sure that your stitches are not going through to the front of the quilt. Repeat for opposite side of quilt.

7. Binding the other two sides: unfold one end of next binding strip and fold in 1/4" on the narrow raw edge; press. Re-fold strip wrong sides together; press. Lay folded-in edge precisely even with outside edge of one of the sewn-on bindings, having the long raw edge of the strip even with the raw edge of unbound side of quilt. Sew with 1/4" seam to within about 2" of other end of quilt. Put needle down into quilt and binding to keep everything from moving around; cut off excess binding 1/4" beyond the bound end of quilt. Tuck in 1/4" seam allowance on (short) raw edge and finish sewing on binding strip. (This binding strip is sewn from edge to edge.) Apply the binding to the opposite side of the quilt the same way.

8. Smooth these two bindings open and fold to back of quilt to just cover stitching line. When you hand sew the last two bindings down, you will probably need to trim out some excess batting and fabric from the corners. Trim a little bit at a time. It's very easy to overtrim and have a wimpy corner. You will have to play with the corners a little to get them to look nice and square and flat—everyone does.

9. And now your quilt is finished! That wasn't so bad was it?

What next?

I hope that you had fun making these Marvelous Mini Quilts and want to make more and more. In my imagination, I can see you playing around with the blocks in this book and finding new sets, recoloring the coloring diagrams in exciting ways and looking at every new block that you see and mentally trying it out.

I.D.—*Do you belong to a Quilt Guild or a Quilt Bee? I think it is so important to stay connected with other quilters—they provide encouragement, enthusiasm and education. I belong to an "On-line" Guild on the GEnie Information Service using my computer and modem, a couple of offline Guilds and a Bee or two. The on-line group lets me keep in touch with other quilters around the country and around the world (we have a member in Okinawa) any time of the day or night. What good friends I have made and I have never met most of them face to face. We swap fabrics and blocks from time to time, have birthday clubs and listen to each other's problems with kids, families, jobs and life in general, as well as "quilt together." In my off-line Guilds, we meet monthly—have a business meeting, an instructional program of some type and (the best part of the meeting) share our quilts in show-and-tell. The Bees are less formal— we sit and stitch and talk and ooh and ah over each other's projects. One Bee meets on Friday mornings; one meets at night on the 22nd of the month regardless of what day of the week it is! So, you see there are quilt groups for everyone! If you haven't yet joined a Guild, do so. If you can't find one, ask at the nearest quilt shop or get a computer and a modem and join us on-line on GEnie .*

Happy quilting!!!